# C. WALTER HODGES

# The Globe

## A STUDY OF THE
## ELIZABETHAN THEATRE

The Norton Library

W·W·NORTON & COMPANY·INC·

NEW YORK

**TO**

# RICHARD SOUTHERN

W. W. Norton & Company, Inc. also publishes *The Norton Anthology of English Literature,* edited by M. H. Abrams et al; *The Norton Anthology of Poetry,* edited by Arthur M. Eastman et al; *World Masterpieces,* edited by Maynard Mack et al; *The Norton Reader,* edited by Arthur M. Eastman et al; *The Norton Facsimile of the First Folio of Shakespeare,* prepared by Charlton Hinman; and the Norton Critical Editions.

Library of Congress Cataloging in Publication Data
Hodges, Cyril Walter, 1909–
   The Globe restored.
   (The Norton library)
   Reprint of the 1968 ed. published by Coward-McCann,
New York.
   Bibliography: p.
   1. Southwark, Eng. Globe Theatre. I. Title.
[PR2920.H6   1973]      792'.09421'64      73-13880
ISBN 0-393-00691-3

Printed in the United States of America
1 2 3 4 5 6 7 8 9 0

# INTRODUCTION

The Elizabethan stage has been a subject of systematic study now for almost a century. Our interest is motivated partly by an antiquarian desire to understand the society of a bygone day, partly by curiosity about the history of theatrical production, partly by a perennial fascination with the plays of Shakespeare. Yet the Elizabethan stage was so different a thing from the stage of our own day, and our information about it has been so fragmentary and so enigmatic, that a concerted effort of the historical imagination is necessary in order to achieve a proper understanding of it. This book is a superlative contribution to such an understanding.

One of the surprising things about the Elizabethan stage is that its technique changed so little during the six-decade life of the "public" and "private" playhouses. To judge from surviving plays, staging was essentially the same at the First Blackfriars Playhouse in the 1580s, at the Globe in the 1600s, and at the Second Blackfriars in the 1630s. This may seem like an implausibly static situation for the theater which made possible so superb and so dynamic a development in the drama—from *Gorboduc* to *The Spanish Tragedy* to *King Lear*, from *Gammer Gurton's Needle* to *Friar Bacon* to *Volpone*—but one should not succumb to the facile assumption of inevitable evolution. Presumably James Burbage, when he built the first permanent Elizabethan playhouse in 1576, wished not to establish a new kind of staging but simply to house traditional methods reaching back through production on booth stages and in temporary hall playhouses during the early sixteenth century to production on pageant-wagons and in circular Place-and-scaffold theaters during the fifteenth century. The Elizabethan stage is better understood not as an opening chapter in the story of the modern picture-frame stage but as a final chapter in the story of the medieval stage. The Elizabethan stage did not "evolve" because it was already, in 1576, a perfected instrument.

"Finis" to that final chapter was writ large and plain in 1642, when all playhouses in England were closed by act of Parliament. The interruption of theatrical tradition was to last for eighteen years. Moreover, upon the Restoration of the Stuart monarchy in 1660 the Elizabethan stage was in effect replaced by a new public stage of changeable scenery (the theater of Dryden and Congreve) in which two framed canvas "shutters" sliding in grooves across the rear of the stage met at the center to form a painted picture or "scene." Early Restoration writers, in retrospect, looked down their noses at the Elizabethan stage, disparaging its "coarse" hangings, "rusty" arras, and "old" tapestry in comparison with the glorious "moveable painted scenes" of modern times. Yet such writers, despite their superiority, must have known what the old stage was.

Not so the writers of a later age. Sometime early in the eighteenth century, with the passing of the Elizabethan stage from living memory, a knowledge of some of its most characteristic features disappeared. Thus by 1790 the great Shakespeare scholar Edmund Malone could suppose, quite as a matter of course, that the Elizabethan stage had a front curtain, for he writes of "the principal curtains that hung in the front of the stage," as distinguished from other, smaller curtains hung at the rear of the stage and used to effect the "discoveries" required by Elizabethan plays. In this astonishing historical error (resulting, clearly, from an unexamined assumption that the Elizabethan stage was in this respect similar to the stage of his own day) Malone was followed by John Payne Collier, who in his monumental history of the English drama published in 1831 writes of "the curtains in front of the stage, and the traverses occasionally drawn and undrawn in the rear of it." But Collier then adds something new, something not found in Malone or earlier writers: the "curtains at the back of the stage . . . served, when drawn, to make another and an inner apartment, when such was required by the business of the play." This appears to be one of the earliest verbal expressions of the idea of an "inner stage" (in the twentieth-century sense of a small proscenium-arch stage, at the rear of a main stage, designed to facilitate the setting of properties out of sight of the audience), as opposed to what we may take to be the Elizabethan reality (a shallow curtained space at the rear of the stage used generally for the occasional discovery of one or two actors). A few years later, in 1836, that idea found concrete expression in the reconstruction of the Fortune Playhouse conceived by Ludwig Tieck and executed by Gottfried Semper which is illustrated and discussed in this book.

Thus began one of the main streams of scholarly tradition flowing into the twentieth century. This tradition led, through the work of Brodmeier, Albright, Godfrey, Thorndike, J. Q. Adams, and others, to the reconstruction of the Globe Playhouse published by John Cranford Adams in 1942. The chief features of this reconstruction are an octagonally shaped playhouse frame, a tapered "outer stage," obliquely set tiring-house doors, an "inner stage," an "upper stage," second-story "window-stages," a third-story music-room, and a system of six trap doors—all of the by-now familiar paraphernalia of the so-called Elizabethan "multiple" stage. It is a fascinating conception, but its practicality has been called in question by experimental productions and historically it appears to derive rather from the theater of Victorian melodrama than from Elizabethan sources of information.

The other major tradition of modern scholarship originates in the discovery by Karl Gaedertz, in 1888, of Arend van Buchell's copy of Johannes de Witt's lost drawing of the interior of the Swan Playhouse. This tradition led, through the work of Ordish, Poel, Reynolds, Lawrence, Forrest, Southern, and others, to the various reconstructions by C. Walter Hodges which, most of them first published in 1953, are the subject of this book. The chief features of these reconstructions are a "round" (that is, polygonal) playhouse frame, a rectangular stage, a tiring-house facade and doors all in a single plane, a tiring house gallery over the stage for the use of both actors and audience (in some cases also a small, projecting "upper stage"), a second-story music-room, a single trap door, and (rather than an "inner stage") a variety of defensible hypotheses in response to the problem posed by the evident need of Elizabethan plays for a "discovery-space."

In this book the reader will find incisive analysis of evidence, flexible and imaginative arguments, an urbane style, a cornucopia of well-chosen pictorial sources, and a series of beautiful drawings by the author which illustrate and clinch the arguments of his text. A better introduction to the Elizabethan playhouse and its stage does not exist—and is not likely to unless C. Walter Hodges writes it.

RICHARD HOSLEY

*Tucson, Arizona*
*June 1973*

# PREFACE TO THE SECOND EDITION

SINCE this book first appeared its field of study has been further surveyed by other writers whose scholarship I cannot pretend to emulate. None the less I am glad to find, in the light of their many studies, that there seems no cause for me to revise the basic propositions within which my book was originally conceived. Rather has the consensus of recent opinion and research tended to confirm my view.

The present edition has been revised, enlarged, and amplified with new illustrations. Moreover, since two critics of the first edition took me to task for not therein venturing upon an actual reconstruction of the Globe, I have here added a new chapter and a drawing which together may be accepted as a contribution to this, even if it does not completely satisfy. I am aware of the dangers; but I find it recognized in the whole field of historical research that this problem is everywhere the same. The historians will always be doubtful of any mere reconstruction of things or events, and strictly speaking may accept nothing beyond the simple, appropriate, and un-interpreted presentation of the hard facts in evidence. Beyond this point it may be said that the understanding of history itself is neither more nor less than a form of personal or corporate fantasy, guided perhaps by wisdom, certainly by changeable tastes and inclinations. But to fill a vacuum, such fantasies will always be supplied. I think therefore that it may be useful for the purposes of the time to supply the best one can.

C. W. H.

*Bishopstone, Sussex*
*1968*

# PREFACE TO THE FIRST EDITION

THE Globe Theatre, which was once a commonplace of the London river-side, and stood in ordinary sun and rain, and grew shabby and had new coats of paint from time to time, and was visited by thousands of people as people nowadays visit the greyhound track or the cinema, has gone forever. Some of its timbers were doubtless sawn up for firewood, some used in the building of other houses, and some two or three, removed again, remain perhaps even to this day built into the wall of a gentleman's week-end cottage in Surrey. But now that the old theatre has been so long demolished, it turns out that there are very few historical buildings of which we would so much wish to have had a reliable record. The problem of reconstructing it has become a fascinating exercise in the field of literary conjecture, the more especially since it is probable that the exact truth about it can never now be known, and that beyond the point where evidence leaves off there is some need, and considerable stimulus, for the imagination. In this book I have tried to strike a proper and declared balance between the facts and my own interpretation of them. No one, I think, is justified in offering a reconstruction of an Elizabethan theatre without insisting upon the neces-sarily conjectural nature of much of it, in view of the limited evidence now available; but if with this caution in mind the reader chooses to accept my findings here, I believe he will find himself somewhere not far from the truth.

I am indebted to many helpers, most particularly to my friend Richard Southern who has allowed me the use not only of his collection of books and pictures but of his researches also, which is generosity indeed. I would like also to acknowledge my thanks to Mr. Walter H. Godfrey, a pioneer in the reconstruction of Elizabethan theatres, who has given me valuable help and advice on many occasions; to Mr. James Laver who has helped me greatly at the Victoria and Albert Museum; to Professor Allardyce Nicoll who as editor of *Shakespeare Survey* first published the article which now appears, with modification, as Chapter 3; and to Bernard and Josephine Miles, in whose garden-house in St. John's Wood many of the pictures in this book were first shown as an exhibition which they helped me to arrange in connexion with the first season of their Mermaid Theatre. I also wish to express thanks to my wife, who has fed, housed, and endured this hobby-horse of mine for some years, and has at last groomed it, typed it, and helped me to send it out into the world.

Among the many books I have consulted, I wish to acknowledge my particular debt to the writings of W. J. Lawrence (*The Physical Features of the Elizabethan Playhouse*, and *Pre-Restoration Stage Studies*); to G. F. Reynolds's *Staging of Elizabethan Plays at the Red Bull Theatre*, which in my view has not yet been equalled as a work of close interpretative analysis on the subject; to John Cranford Adams's *The Globe Theatre, its Design and Equipment*; to George R. Kernodle's *From Art to Theatre*; and of course to the four invaluable volumes of Sir E. K. Chambers's *The Elizabethan Stage*. And being conscious of all the earlier work by other men, I can only offer as my excuse for coming in at this point the following, from John Speed's Preface to his *Theatre of the Empire of Great Britain*:

I stand in suspense, so many maister-builders having in this subject gone before me, and I the least, not worthy to hew (much less to lay) the least stone in so beautiful a Building; neither can I for my heedless presumption alledge any excuse, unless it be this, that . . . I knew not what I undertook until I saw the charges thereof by others bestowed to amount so high as I held it a conscience to frustrate their designments; wherein albeit it may be objected I have put my sickle into other men's corn and have laid my building upon other men's foundations . . . yet this in part sufficeth for my defence, that in the work of the Tabernacle there was more mettals used than orient gold, and more workmen employed than Aholiab and Bezaleel.

C. W. H.

*Bishopstone, Sussex*
*1953*

# CONTENTS

From the Fables of Phaedrus, Amsterdam, 1688

# LIST OF ILLUSTRATIONS

## PLATES

The plates inserted between pages 144–5

## LINE DRAWINGS IN THE TEXT

Unless otherwise stated drawings in the text are by the author

# I. THE RUINS OF PALMYRA

FOR the space of nearly seventy years, from the latter half of the reign of Elizabeth the First until the time of the Civil War, there flourished in London no less that fifteen theatres. Some of these, calling themselves private theatres, were built indoors for the comfortable entertainment of fairly small and select audiences; but the rest, nine altogether, were public places built rather like small Roman amphitheatres, open to the sky, and each capable of holding about two thousand spectators. Nothing quite like them had been known in Europe since the days of the Roman Empire, and not for more than another two hundred years was there any other city which could show so many permanent theatres at one time. The name of one of these will remain illustrious so long as there is any history of theatres at all. It is that of Shakespeare's theatre, the Globe.

We have details of more than twenty actors' companies who worked in the theatres of Elizabethan and Jacobean London, and of these nearly five hundred individual actors are known to us by name—some, like Alleyn, Burbage, Field, Armin, Kempe, and Tarlton, by much more than name. We know from the documents that have come down to us, the details of their management and organization, of their legal and business affairs, and especially of their plays. Wide and crowded shelves make up the library of surviving Elizabethan plays, good, bad, and brilliant, from the pens of more than a dozen famous dramatists, without counting Marlowe, Jonson, or Shakespeare. If the theatres were the first of their kind since Roman times, there had been nothing to compare with this fountain of playwriting since the days of Periclean Athens. It is therefore the more remarkable that with all this residue of fame and knowledge to guide us, we are today more uncertain about the actual stagecraft employed in the original production of one of Shakespeare's plays at the Globe than we are of any other event of comparable importance in the whole history of the theatre.

This is not to say that we know nothing: we know much about it—but it is widely believed that we know much more than we do; for where knowledge ends conjectures have been accepted to fill the unacceptable gap; and many of these conjectures, like old friends, have grown to be received without question.

Knowledge on the subject is most extensive over its peripheral areas. For example, we are pretty well informed about audiences at the Globe and how they behaved there, or about the cost of an actor's wardrobe, or of getting a poet released from prison, and so on. It is when we seek for reliable information about the centre of all this, the stage itself and how it was used, that the evidence suddenly becomes obscure on many points, and on others is altogether lacking. For example, there are in existence authentic contracts which give what at first appear to be full details for the building of two of the theatres, the Fortune and the Hope; but the Hope contract, when it comes to the point where it should describe the stage, which is the thing above all which we wish to have described, tells us nothing except that it was built on trestles so that it could easily be taken down; and the Fortune contract, having stated that the details of its stage are to be copied from the Globe, at that point purports to append a diagram of it, to make all clear. That diagram, alas, has not survived. Had it done so, it might have saved a whole world of ink and paper which has since tried to replace it.

It is my purpose in this book to bring together a collection of evidence, and especially of pictures related to the subject, which, together with some personal opinions and reconstructions of my own, will create a visual impression of the style and manner of the London theatre in the time of Shakespeare. And since for most people today this means the Globe, we shall do well to take the Globe for the centre and model of our subject.

There were two versions of the Globe. The first was built on Bankside in Southwark in 1599, and enjoyed a successful career until 1613, when it was accidentally burned down during a play which, from its description, we take to be Shakespeare's *Henry VIII*. The second was built to replace it on the same site, and was opened the following year. The management took the occasion to improve on their former building, and a certain John Chamberlain wrote in a letter to a friend that he heard 'much speech of this new playhouse, which is said to be the fairest that ever was in England'. This second building continued on Bankside until 1644, when, what with the ground-lease falling in, the Civil War in progress, the Puritans in the ascendant, and the old theatres out of fashion anyway, it was finally pulled down. Its near neighbour, which had once been the Hope Theatre, but which had long since reverted to an older calling as a bear-baiting arena (it is shown in all the old maps as a 'Bear-garden'), survived it for only a few more years. It was demolished in 1656. Its site is still marked by an alley called Bear Gardens; and next door to it is another, Rose Alley, which marks the site of a yet older theatre, the Rose. The Globe stood a short way to the east and south of this, and the whole group as it existed in 1600 can be seen in a newly discovered revised version of Norden's map of London, the Bankside portion of which is shown in Plate 2. This is now considered to be the most reliable of all the old maps of Bankside, but even so the Rose is wrongly named in it, being here called the Star. The mistake may have arisen because a heraldic rose, if seen indistinctly, could easily be confused with a heraldic star. The mistake is in any case typical of many which have confused research on the siting of these theatres. There is no room here to describe the difficulties which for a long time obstructed the search for the lost site of the Globe itself, but it is relevant to note that in the course of it it was necessary to establish firstly, that an old map, vital to the evidence, had actually been drawn upside down, and secondly, that in a famous engraving, Hollar's 'Long View of London', which shows the Globe and the Bear-garden as they were shortly before the Civil War (Plate 4), the titles of these two theatres had accidentally been interchanged, the Globe being named 'Beere bayting' and vice versa. The site of the Globe has now been established beyond reasonable doubt, and those two unlikely-seeming propositions have been proved to be correct; but it can well be imagined that many experts found them difficult to accept, and that research was confused as a consequence.

A similar confusion and controversy still exists as to the actual shape of the Globe. Shakespeare called it a 'wooden O', but it is contended that if it had been a fully rounded O it was not likely, for structural reasons, to have been made all of wood. It is possible that the outer wall was circular, composed of some sort of flint and mortar concrete, like the Keep at the Tower of London, and it has to be noted that de Witt's account of the Swan described that theatre as being 'built of a concrete of flint stones' (see p. 108, below). However, in a letter to his nephew, describing the burning of the first Globe two days after the event, Sir Henry Wotton wrote that 'the whole house' was burned to the ground, and that 'nothing did perish but wood and straw'; and Ben Jonson, in his poem on that occasion, 'An Execration Upon Vulcan', stated that there was 'nothing but the piles left'. Had there been a concrete shell much of this must have remained standing. Hollar's engraving of the Second Globe (Plate 5) certainly shows a smooth, round exterior like a concrete building; but the Visscher engraving (Plate 1) shows an emphatically polygonal structure. To me it seems reasonably certain that the First Globe, and probably the Second also, was a timber-framed polygon. If the polygon had been constructed with sixteen sides, this from a little distance would have appeared as a full round, and when Hollar made the original sketch for his engraving from the tower of St. Saviour's Church (now Southwark Cathedral) he would certainly have found it convenient to draw it so (Plate 5). But whatever doubts there may be about this detail, there ought to be none about the quality of Hollar's picture as a whole. It is the only single picture of the Bankside playhouses which we can confidently accept as a good and reliable representation. The only question is whether there had been any substantial alterations made between Shakespeare's time and the time when Hollar made his drawing. There is no real reason to suppose so.

As soon as regular playgoing was resumed in London at the Restoration, the old-time theatres were remembered with some contempt. 'Now for the difference between our Theatres and those of former times,' wrote one Restoration commentator,[1] 'they were but plain and simple, with no Scenes, nor Decorations of the Stage, but onely old Tapestry, and the Stage strewed with rushes (with their Habits accordingly).' This was a view of the Elizabethan theatre which was to prevail for more than two hundred years thereafter, that it was a poor barnyard affair, picturesque but crude. The rush-strewn stage and the lack of movable picture-scenery could not help but seem a great drawback to the new generation of playgoers for whom the splendid scenic inventions which had been introduced into this country by Inigo Jones a generation before, at the court of James I, were now being shown regularly on the public stage. 'Scenes' were the rage, and such of the Elizabethan plays as were thought suitable for revival were now altered to suit the scenic style. Shakespeare's were among the first to be adapted. Pepys wrote in his diary that he had been to see 'Hamlet done with scenes very well'. So the old theatres had gone not only unregretted but unremembered. Moreover, they had suffered the fate of so many commonplace and popular institutions, that everybody had taken them for granted and nobody had put them on record. Such inadequate records as we have date from their early days, when they were novelties; but of their later professional and routine years we have hardly any account at all.

There remained, however, the printed plays, especially the plays of Shakespeare, and as time went on it began to be necessary for editors to explain those technical peculiarities which, under the now well-settled system of the scenic theatres, seemed increasingly ill suited to what had become the normal stage requirements. For example, how had Shakespeare intended the rapid succession of short scenes in Act IV of *Antony and Cleopatra* to be

[1] Richard Flecknoe, *Discourse of the English Stage* (1664).

presented? Or what does Cassius mean in Act V of *Julius Caesar* when he instructs Pindarus to 'get higher on that hill'? And when *Pindarus goes up*, up on what in fact does he go? Then in *Henry VIII*, II. ii, after a scene between the Lord Chamberlain and the Dukes of Norfolk and Suffolk, a stage direction says: *Exit Lord Chamberlain; and the King draws the curtain and sits reading pensively*; but what curtain is here referred to? The 'doors' which are so often alluded to, as in *Cymbeline*, VII, where *Enter . . . the Roman Army at one door and the Briton Army at another*, might perhaps have made sense to an eighteenth-century reader whose stage still contained, by tradition, two fixed doors in the proscenium; but nevertheless he might have thought it a curious use of such doors. But then, turning from Shakespeare to Field's *A Woman's a Weathercock*, the eighteenth-century reader might have been even more hard put to it to make sense out of the stage direction: *Scudmore passeth one door and entereth the other, where Bellafront sits in a Chair, under a Taffeta Canopy*. Such references to contemporary stage conditions could perhaps be explained away as the quaint makeshifts of a bygone age, but even so it was not altogether clear what they were making shift to do.

Meanwhile certain old engravings of Bankside had been copied and copied again, one from another, and the strange tub-shaped buildings which were to be seen in the foregrounds of most of them became stranger and stranger as the debasement of copies went on (cf. Plates 8 and 9). Antiquarians and literary people in the eighteenth century puzzled over them; but if ever they went over to Bankside in search of grounds more relative than this, they must have been disappointed; though Mrs. Thrale indeed believed that she had seen the actual remains of the Globe itself. Her husband, Henry Thrale, had established his brewery on Bankside upon a site which is still occupied by a brewery today, and which, according to local tradition at that time, included the site of the Globe. Mrs. Thrale wrote of it afterwards, in her memoirs:

For a long time, then—or I thought it such—my fate was bound up with the old Globe Theatre, upon the Bankside, Southwark; the alley it had occupied having been purchased and thrown down by Mr Thrale to make an opening before the windows of our dwelling-house. When it lay desolate in a black heap of rubbish, my Mother, one day, in a joke, called it the Ruins of Palmyra; and after that they laid it down in a grass-plot. Palmyra was the name it went by, I suppose, among the clerks and servants of the brewhouse. . . .

But there were really curious remains of the old Globe Playhouse, which though hexagonal in form without, was round within.

Yet she was wrong, after all. Her Palmyra was not the ruin of the Globe, but of some old tenements a little way off to the south of it, which were demolished in 1767, just about the time she went to live in Southwark. As for the true site, she and her husband must have walked over it in the brewery many times. Her observations about the shape of the Globe, hexagonal without and round within, are open to doubt on many grounds, and one must suppose she was quoting from a mixed memory of Shakespeare's 'wooden O' speech and the Visscher engraving.

In a similar vein, there was published in 1811 an engraving by Shepherd which purported to be of 'The Fortune Playhouse, Golden Lane'. It shows nothing but a tumbledown row of old shops, glorified with a coat of arms, but ready to crumble into another Palmyra within the next few years. Clearly, any connexion between this building and of the Fortune Playhouse must have been extremely remote, and certainly, the small area given to the supposed playhouse in an appended map cannot have been correct. But the memory of the old theatre still floated about over the place, and roused enough interest among educated people to make the publication of a print worth while (Plate 10).

Though the Globe was lost, there were certain critics in the latter part of the eighteenth century who, in spite of the well-developed amenities of the theatres of their own time, were prepared to believe that the stagecraft of Shakespeare's day deserved investigation. In the Introduction to his 1768 edition of Shakespeare, Edward Capell wrote: 'Even the stage he [Shakespeare] appeared upon, its form, dressings, actors should be enquired into, as every one of those circumstances had some considerable effect upon what he composed for it.' This suggestion was taken up by Edmund Malone a few years later, and it was he whose researches into the Henslowe documents, the Revels accounts, and other contemporary records, laid the foundations upon which all the subsequent work of reconstruction was based.

Throughout the nineteenth century the features of the lost Globe were diligently hunted in texts and documents, and, where these failed, in the realm of conjectural inspiration. The study of it, so rich in colour and so fruitful of interesting detail, proved to be as baffling as it was attractive.

However, an answer was provided bit by bit, and if we now think that it erred too far upon the side of the primitive, this was only in keeping with the then prevailing belief in the general progress of cultured man out of medieval backwardness towards Victorian enlightenment. Besides, the evidence of the condition of the Elizabethan theatre did much to confirm this view. What else could one think of a theatre where the roof was of thatch, and where, while a part of the audience was expected to stand on a winter's afternoon under an open sky, another part was allowed to sit smoking and playing cards upon the stage, interrupting the play at will? And had not Shakespeare himself described his theatre as a 'cockpit', a 'wooden O', and an 'unworthy scaffold', lamenting the conditions which were to reduce his Agincourt to the scale of 'four or five most vile and ragged foils, right ill-disposed in brawl ridiculous'? If such, then, were really the customs of the Elizabethan playhouse (and no one suggests that they were not, though we may wonder to what degree this applied), it is fair to ask whether it has been worth while to take so much trouble to reconstruct so simple a thing. But the point is that it has always been suspected, and for good reasons, that the evidence that has survived, unassailable though it is as to detail *within* the subject, is in fact not typical of the character of the subject *as a whole*: the evidence is very much concerned with picturesque oddities which were noted at the time simply because they were odd and picturesque. The work of research has been to find the truth which lay behind them.

The desire to collect and restore the relics of past time, to re-create the features of history, to establish and guard them in the air-conditioned permanence of libraries, museums, and art galleries, is one of the characteristic impulses of our age. It is, I suppose, a form of ancestor-worship. It seems to promise us the security of our own memorials in the future, since the tribute which we thus pay to our forefathers we may expect to be repaid to ourselves, when our time comes to be forefathers. The piecing-together of the Globe is only a part of the general piecing-together which, from the days of the eighteenth-century antiquarians until now, has thoroughly restored to us a whole world of reference of our past. It has been found all the more exasperating, therefore, that, considering the veneration given to Shakespeare, it has been so difficult to collect the working details of his stage—or, for that matter, of his own life. This has not only been a goad to research but has, moreover, provided its own pleasures in the game of conjectural detection. But there is more to it than this. The relics and curiosities which former antiquaries collected are now seen for what they are: not, that is, as 'curiosities' at all, but as mature examples of artistic styles which, although they may be unlike our own, are usually every inch as good, and sometimes better. So it is with the Elizabethan theatre. I do not think it can be claimed that as a theatre it was any better than our own, though in most respects it was as good. The question of comparative quality is not the point, however. The point is that the presentations of the Elizabethan theatre were expressed in an artistic style which was different from ours, and which was largely abandoned in favour of the scenery theatre, not because it was essentially inferior to it, but because at a time of transition the scenery theatre had all the glamour of aristocratic taste and of magic novelty to back it up. This has now been developed to the point where further progress is hardly to be imagined. The Elizabethan style, however, still remains to be explored and developed from where it left off, and contains, fully ripened and ready for planting, the seeds of a different kind of theatrical experience from the one we are accustomed to. It is because of its abiding artistic potency that people in the theatre, ever since Benjamin Webster's attempt to reconstruct the original staging of *The Taming of the Shrew* in 1844, and especially since the famous experiments of William Poel and his company at the St. George's Hall in 1881 and with the Elizabethan Stage Society thereafter, have so often been ready to try putting the Elizabethan method into practice; and it has been for this reason rather more than for the picturesque braggadocio of its historical colour that the restoration of the Globe has been so much advocated. But what has yet to be decided is the character which such a restoration ought to have.

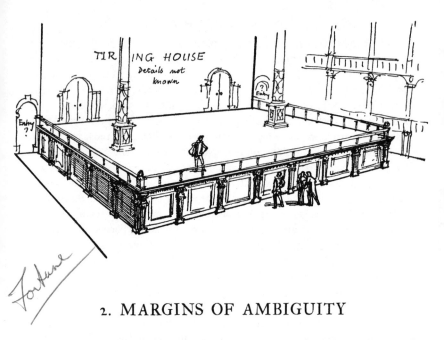

TIRING HOUSE
Details not
known

Entry
?

Entry
?

Entry
?

Fortune

## 2. MARGINS OF AMBIGUITY

I HAVE suggested already that the Victorian belief in straight-line progress from the Middle Ages onwards had led to over-simplification in the problem of the Globe. It has also led, among other things, to the assumption that our modern kind of theatre originated in the Elizabethan one, and that by tracing backwards from eighteenth-century and Restoration theatres one would find their embryonic form at the Globe. This in its turn has led to a belief, which is to be discussed in another chapter, that the modern proscenium arch developed out of an Elizabeth 'inner stage'. But even that 'inner stage' itself is more of a nineteenth-century supposition than an Elizabethan fact. According to W. J. Lawrence, it was first suggested by Ludwig Tieck, the great German editor and translator of Shakespeare, in the course of an historical novel.[1] The trouble about the straight-line progress

[1] See illustration at Plate 11, and the Note on it, pp. 112–14.

idea was that it did not take into account the possibility that the Restoration stage was arrived at more by deliberate invention than by historical development, and that the Elizabethan public theatre was principally the repository of a great medieval tradition of stagecraft which was not handed on, but fizzled out on Bankside in the years after Shakespeare's death, while the new stagecraft, fortified with the new scenic methods, was developed in the other, indoor, playhouses. But, needless to say, if we trace back from Restoration practices to the Globe, we shall miss altogether this medieval element, which was so important a part of its character. The early restorers did not omit the medieval reference from their calculations, but they tended to give it a wrong emphasis; they allowed it to be a factor in the auditorium, but not much in the stagecraft: they allowed that it formed a part of the Elizabethan literary inheritance, but owing, perhaps, to their concentration on Shakespeare's work rather than on the great number of inferior plays which represent the more normal, run-of-the-mill tastes of the time, they assumed that it faded early from the scene, whereas it seems evident to many critics nowadays that it did not.

The practices of the modern stage are constant, almost universal. They work consistently within its accepted frame of scenic, lighting, orchestral, and managerial arrangements, to such an extent that even the most rustic of amateur dramatic societies would consider itself naked and untutored if it could not provide itself with some sort of attempt at the curtain-and-lighting arrangements of a 'proper theatre'. But the Elizabethan company of players did not fashion its style upon the acceptance of any particular structure. The Chamberlain's Men of the Globe were well housed in their up-to-date building, but their plays and methods were such that they could be taken straight from there into the countryside, or into the Queen's banqueting hall, with hardly a change, in just the same way that Peter Quince and his men could first make 'this green plot . . . our stage, this hawthorne-brake our tiring house', and then go from there into the palace of Duke Theseus to give their performance. The character of the modern stage is rooted in the technical machinery that houses it and provides its effects. But the Elizabethan theatre was portable, self-contained, adjustable, and independent of any surroundings other than its audience. The very stage itself needed to be no more than an open floor, which was only raised up for the better convenience of the spectators. And although we may find that the Elizabethans did make use in their fixed theatres of certain structural features which we interpret as having formed a part of their permanent stage building—e.g. an 'upper stage'—we ought not to suppose that every similar case refers of necessity to the same thing. We ought to leave space in our interpretations for variability and improvisation. The attempt to reconstruct Elizabethan theatres as though they were all permanently uniform, and a belief that the stage directions in plays, and some random textual references to stage conditions, all refer uniformly to certain permanent structural features which were to be found at all the theatres, surely ought not to be carried too far. It is a typically modern and 'technical' approach, of the kind which has in the past helped bring about some very dubious theories as to the whole nature of Elizabethan stagecraft. There was, for example, Carl Brodmeier's 'alternation' theory, now generally discredited. According to this the Elizabethans constructed their plays so as to allow the scenes to be acted alternately between the front and rear portions of the stage, which was divided, Brodmeier asserted, by a curtain suspended between the two great stage pillars. In this way the Elizabethans could be brought into line with the modern technique of changing stage furniture and properties unseen behind curtains. Another more up-to-date and rather more complex theory assumes that the architecture of the Elizabethan stage was specially designed to allow for action to take place around a number of permanent structural units at different levels, such as on upper floors or at fixed doors and windows, and that plays were written with this complex stage in mind. Such methods, excellent to the modern mind, are not at all in the character of the Elizabethan one. Moreover, if such a theory as that last mentioned were true, it would imply that the Elizabethan actors had invented a form of stagecraft different from anything known before, which had no family connexion with any other theatrical style of its time, and which, in spite of its success in its own time, was eventually abandoned altogether. Such an isolated phenomenon would be unlikely in the world of the theatre at any time, and especially in the sixteenth century. Theatrical people have always been great respecters of traditional practices. Surely it would be far better to assume that the style of the Elizabethan theatre was based on tradition, and that it developed in accordance with the accepted theatrical modes of its day, not only the English mode, but that of the Netherlands, Germany, France, and Italy also.

Here again the early critics were at a disadvantage, for there was little or no comparative theatrical history for them to draw upon. Before quite recent times the history of the theatre was confined (except for the memoirs of famous actors) to the history of dramatic *literature*, which is a rather different thing. All the ornate and gorgeous theatrical pomps of the Renaissance, all the popular jig-stuff, all the farces of the Italian Comedians, all the scenic ingenuities of Torelli, the Bibienas, and Bérain, having no great literature to back them up, were considered to have no place for serious consideration. They existed only as drawings and engravings which most critics thought of as fantasies perhaps not seriously intended even for the stage. And for a long time there were no pictures at all of the interior of an Elizabethan theatre. The nearest examples known were on the title-pages of two Caroline-published plays, Alabaster's *Roxana* and Richards's *Messallina* (Plates 49 and 50), and these, apart from the fact that they each showed a prow-like stage backed by curtains, were not much help. Another picture, the frontispiece to Kirkman's *The Wits* (see p. 30), showed the same kind of thing applying to a popular performance in Restoration times, evidently indoors; but this again was not much to go upon. Then in 1888 the German critic Karl Gaedertz published a drawing which he had found in the University Library of Utrecht. It showed an authentic view of the interior of the Swan Theatre in London (Plate 3), which from associated evidence can be dated to about the year 1596. The drawing tallies remarkably with the independent evidence of the old exterior views. It has the rounded house, the hut, and the flag. It shows also that 'shadow or cover' over the stage, supported by posts, which are features mentioned in the Hope and Fortune contracts, already referred to. But because it does not show a curtained recess at the rear of the stage, and is ambiguously if not badly drawn in other places, it has been sometimes criticized as an unsound foundation upon which to build. It is pointed out that it is a report at second hand, being a copy by one man of an original sketch by another. Indeed, it may have been done only from a verbal description, with no previous drawing at all. But, however that may be, one of the two men concerned in it had in fact visited London and had in fact seen the Swan Theatre, and, as already noted, his evidence tallies exactly with other evidence we have. The drawing, then, whatever its faults and difficulties, must form, as Sir Edmund Chambers has said, 'the inevitable basis of any comprehensive account of the main structural features of a playhouse'. If we differ from it (as most reconstructions do, to some extent), it can only be either because we believe in the variability of the playhouses one from another, or else because we consider the picture faulty in some detail or other of draughtsmanship. But if evidence is to have any value at all we are not at liberty to differ from it very widely.

The publication of the Swan drawing enabled scholars to agree at last upon a general representative reconstruction of an Elizabethan playhouse, which, although still only conjectural, could be offered as a good basis for the understanding of Shakespearian methods of production. All the evidence which had been so diligently assembled and studied for so long was now gathered in, so to speak, under the roof of the Swan and arranged to fit into the Swan framework. The result was a synthetic but very acceptable picture. In the following chapters of this book I propose to criticize it from certain angles, but chiefly with a view to adjusting it and perhaps adding to it here and there, if I can, and not with any idea of trying to disintegrate what has been so usefully put together. First, however, let us examine the picture as we find it, noting what features of it are certain, and what are conjectural.

It is certain that the Elizabethan playgoer, when he approached one of the big public playhouses to see the afternoon's show, came in most cases to a round building (and I shall allow the word 'round' to include polygonal, since this gives the same general impression, as opposed to a rectangular building). Built over the top of this round house was a hut, usually quite small (though in Hollar's engraving it is large), and over the hut there waved a flag. As he went in at the door he paid his money into a box, which was held by one of the playhouse staff called a 'gatherer'. This money allowed him to enter the open yard where stood the stage, and around the yard, overlooking the stage, three tiers of galleries were built up. (Three tiers are certain, at any rate, at the Fortune, the Hope, and the Swan, which strongly indicate the same for the Globe and all the rest.) What we are not quite certain about is the arrangement of the main entrance doors. The

Swan drawing shows none, and the inference is that it is placed centrally, facing the stage and below the station point from which the drawing purports to have been done. This is the supposition upon which all reconstructions are made, I think without exception. It is worth bearing in mind, however, that the First Globe had two doors. Sir Ralph Winwood, in a contemporary letter in which he referred to the burning-down of that building, remarked that 'it was a great marvaile . . . that the people had so little harm, having but two narrow doors to get out'. This is usually interpreted as referring to the public entrance on the one hand and the tiring-house or actors' entrance on the other. That interpretation may be right, but it is still worth questioning whether the letter-writer had not in his mind's eye the normal means of public access, which is what his words sound like, without thinking of the tiring-house door round at the back—if that is where it was. Besides, it is a most usual and common-sense axiom at public auditoriums that there must always be more doors for people to go out from a play, which they do in a crowd at the end, than for their coming in, which they do in ones and twos at the beginning. If, then, the doors were narrow, as Sir Ralph Winwood says, it would be reasonable to assume that there were two *public doors*, one only being used for entrance, but both being flung open at the end of the show. And if there were two doors they would most likely have been placed not facing but flanking the stage and opposite to each other. In some of the black-and-white sketches in this book I have suggested this arrangement for what it is worth; and I think it is at least worth bearing in mind.[1]

It appears that the entrances to the auditorium galleries led up out of the yard. At any rate, the Swan drawing seems to indicate this, and a scandalized person, writing in 1582,[2] declared that 'in the playhouses at London, it is the fashion of youthes to go first into the yarde, and there to carry their eye through every gallery' seeking for women to whom, when they see them, 'they flye, and presse as nere to ye fairest as they can'. He goes on to

[1] However, an engraving of the Curtain playhouse (Plate 7), which has been brought to light by Dr. Leslie Hotson since the above was written, does show an entrance door where it has always been supposed, centrally facing the stage. It is the only picture which actually shows this. It does make the matter pretty certain, though I am still inclined to think the two-door theory may be considered as a possible variant at some theatres, such as the Fortune (see Appendix A, fig. 6).

[2] Stephen Gosson, *Plays Confuted in Five Actions* (1582).

say that 'they give them pippines, they dally with their garments, to pass ye time'. However, it seems they got to these pastimes by way of the yard, and it is known that in going from one part of the house to another they would be required to pay varying supplementary charges at the entrances to different divisions of the house. If they were poor they paid their penny for first entrance and went no further than the yard, where they stood among the groundlings. If they were well-to-do and privileged they might take the 'Lords' rooms' or one of the 'gentlemen's rooms' which are variously described as 'over' or 'next to' the stage. For a fuller discussion of the auditorium with its penny and twopenny galleries and its 'twelve-penny rooms', the reader is referred to John Cranford Adams's book, *The Globe Playhouse*, though it should here be noted that Adams does not agree that the galleries were reached by way of the yard.

Now that he has entered and taken his place, the playgoer faces a stage which is familiar to him from whatever place or angle he may be viewing it; for he has often been here before, and the stage has always been the same. It is useful to remember this when considering the matter of the visibility of scenes on the Elizabethan stage. Their playhouses were not planned according to a scientific layout based on sight-lines as our modern theatres are, and visibility must have been bad from many parts of a house which was as prolific in posts and pillars as we know the Elizabethan playhouse to have been. But good visibility, essential in a modern theatre, which relies so much upon the effects of changeable scenery, is hardly of first importance, important though it may still be, in a theatre whose features are fixed, known, and expected from one visit to the next.

The stage, as we know, was thrust out from one side of the surrounding house into the centre of the yard, like a great wooden peninsula. Of its shape, there is some question whether it was rectangular or tapering, but this and other matters concerned with the stage itself we are to discuss separately in Chapter 3. We shall also leave until later most of our consideration of the area around and within the house-wall at the back of the stage, the area called the tiring-house. Some points about it may be noted here, however. It is agreed in nearly all reconstructions that the interior of the tiring-house on the stage level was divided off from the stage by hangings of some sort, usually curtains opening in the middle. Contemporary texts sometimes mention curtains and sometimes arras, and it is worth-while to note that the two are not necessarily the same: an arras usually suggests a fixed hanging, or a tapestry, which cannot be drawn aside like a curtain. Therefore if the opening at the rear of the stage should be hung with arras, one could make an entrance from it by lifting a flap of it at the sides or middle, but could not part it in such a way as to make the space behind it usable as a supplementary stage. But this could, of course, be done if the opening were hung with curtains, which could be drawn aside on rings.[1]

We will accept, then, for the time being, an opening at the back, which could be hung with either arras or curtains (although the Swan drawing does not show this). We will accept also the convention that on each side of this opening were two doors, such as are shown in the Swan drawing. We will agree that these doors may have been a part of an Elizabethan stage practice which was carried over to later times, being perhaps the prototypes of the famous apron-stage doors of the Restoration theatres; but we should note in passing that the convention which allows us to imagine only a single pair of stage doors for every type of Elizabethan stage has to reckon with a certain number of contradictory stage directions, such as, *Enter three in black clokes, at three doores*, from the *Four Prentices of London*. Perhaps there was a third door at the back within the opening, which is the solution usually given; but one would be at liberty, so far as hard evidence is concerned, to make a reconstruction envisaging three or more doors if one wished to do so. Neither, of necessity, need such doors be large. There is an argument that they would have to be large enough to allow the entrance of spectacular processional objects such as Tamburlaine's chariot and the cage of Bajazet in Marlowe's *Tamburlaine*. But it is equally if not more likely that such things would be brought in through the central hangings, when there were any, as they are through the hangings at the ring entrance of any travelling circus today. Of course, the Swan drawing does show large doors; but in this case there are no hangings.

[1] References to 'drawing an arras' do, however, exist. In *The Booke of Sir Thomas Moore*, for instance, there is the stage direction: *An Arras is drawne, and behind it (as in Sessions) sit the L. Mayor, Justice Suresbie . . ., etc.* Still, the word 'curtain' is far more usual in this situation, and it has been necessary to point out the distinction between these two types of hanging, the one of light sarcenet, easily drawn aside on rings, the other fixed, of canvas or some similar material made heavier with painting, to represent tapestry.

So much, then, until a later chapter, about the features of the stage rear
wall. Let us now turn to the stage itself, and consider those two great
posts which, according to the evidence of the Swan drawing, stood out
upon it. For most people these represent more than any other thing the
curious character of the Elizabethan stage. And at once the problem of
visibility comes again into the question. How could such a pair of pillars
be placed as the Swan drawing shows them to be, and not impair visibility,
especially of anything taking place on the rear part of the stage? The
answer must be that the pillars *did* impair visibility, but to what extent
they did so would depend upon their exact placing and upon the amount
of use made of the rear parts of the stage. I think myself that modern commentators have tended to put far too much stress upon this area at the
back, and that the general tendency was for the actors to come right out
into the forward parts, near to the most central point of the surrounding
audience. But there the pillars stood, and it is generally agreed that the
actors sometimes made use of them, as is found in Haughton's *Englishmen
for my Money*, where two characters, supposed to be groping their way
along in the dark, bump into them one after the other, and presently
declare them to be a couple of maypoles. Most commentators seem to
think that these pillars were conventionally used to represent trees, and
that when characters were supposed to climb a tree, as in Jonson's *The Case
is Altered*, IV. iv, where a stage direction says that the character Onion does
so, they somehow climbed up this pillar, or some part of it, such as on to
the plinth. It is also supposed that the cutpurses whom 'we tye to a poast
on our stage, for all people to wonder at, when at a play they are taken
pilfring'[1] were tied to one of these. I cannot agree with either of these
assumptions. There is no way of climbing these pillars that could be either
convenient or effective. It is far more reasonable to suppose that these cases
refer to the use of other, smaller posts, probably at the rear of the stage
against the tiring-house, where a character could climb up into a 'tree' at
the first gallery level. Any sort of elaboration of the tiring-house façade
in the Elizabethan style is likely to have produced ornamental pillars, and
we know that at the Hope, where there were definitely no pillars at all
supporting the roof-canopy over the stage (which was the function of those

[1] William Kempe, *Nine Days' Wonder* (1660)

at the Swan), there were none the less some 'turned columns upon and over the stage'. The meaning of this is not clear, but in its context it seems to me to indicate pillars against the tiring-house façade.

I have said above 'there the pillars stood'; but it is proper to point out that they have not stood unquestioned, except for the unquestionable case of the Swan. Dr. A. M. Nagler in his study of the subject[1] has rejected them as doubtful in common practice. He writes:

> It is doubtful whether the stages of the Theatre, the Curtain, or the Globe had two lofty posts like those supporting the stage roof in the Swan sketch. . . . The Fortune contract mentions no stage posts, though it does call for a 'shadow'. In any case, the Hope Playhouse had no vertical roof supports, for the contractor was requested to 'builde the Heavens all over the saide stage to be borne or carryed without any postes or supporters to be fixed or sett vppon the said stage'. The specification was necessary in this case, because in other respects the Hope was a copy of the Swan, which did have roof supports. Therefore, it is unreasonable to assume that the Fortune had such supports simply because the contract does not expressly preclude them. The Fortune was built on the model of the Globe, just as the Hope was built on the model of the Swan. It is more logical to conclude that neither the Fortune nor the Globe had roof supports. The Swan was perhaps the exception.

I respect this argument, but ultimately I do not feel able to accept it. The problem devolves, after all, upon the function of these pillars. They were there, as the Swan drawing shows, to support the roof-canopy and hut-like building overhanging the stage, which together were generally called the 'Heavens'. (The Fortune contract calls the roof a 'shadow or cover'.) The purpose of these will be discussed below: but here we must pause to emphasize that this hut-like unit standing within and above the enclosure of the main playhouse building is a dominant feature of *all* the main exterior views of Elizabethan public playhouses except one, the Hope, for which, as we have seen in Nagler's quotation, special provision was made to do away with stage posts. I have attempted in a sketch (given at Appendix A, fig. 7) to show how I think this may have been done in such a way as to give the effect recorded in Hollar's engraving (Plate 4). Meanwhile, if the hutted type of Heavens was in fact usual, as the other engravings show, then it is difficult to see how, within the means commonly available to Elizabethan builders, they could have been supported, if not by posts.

[1] *Shakespeare's Stage* (New Haven, 1958).

Since I find that the Swan sketch and the various exterior views, independently drawn, corroborate each other; and since, with the evidence as it is
at present, I feel obliged to accept Chambers's view that the Swan sketch
must form 'the inevitable basis of any comprehensive account . . . of a playhouse', I do not feel able to accept Nagler's doubts on the point. I choose
rather to accept the posts.

I have dwelt rather long (some may think over-long) upon the subject
of these posts because it is connected with an argument I wish to put forward in a later chapter, when we shall return to the matter of the stage
rear wall, the façade of the tiring-house. But here and now we pass on to
consider the hut and roof of the Heavens, which the stage posts supported.

The function of that forward pent-roof over half the stage which we see
in the Swan drawing must have been to give partial shelter in unsettled
weather, to prevent a play from being interrupted by a short shower of rain.
(On very wet days, of course, there would be no performances.) But the
hut which stood, so typical a feature, up above all the rest of the theatre,
was clearly the place where was housed the hoisting machinery which
raised and lowered the cloud-wreathed thrones and chariots of gods and
magicians between the Heavens and the stage. Seen from below, the underside of the hut and of the 'shadow' roof, would most proably have presented a fine spectacle of ornamental painting. It has been pointed out by
T. S. Graves[1] that there are many references in plays of the period which
suggest there was some sort of ornamental zodiac motif painted in the
upper regions over the stage. This has been generally accepted, and in his
*From Art to Theatre* (p. 96) G. R. Kernodle reproduces a picture of a
sixteenth-century ceiling painted in just this way. Another such ceiling
is shown here at Plate 61.

In the midst of the painted ceiling there was a trapdoor through which,
when it was opened, the 'creaking throne comes down, the boyes to please',
as Ben Jonson described it in the Prologue to *Every Man In His Humour*.
The creaking, if there was any (for Jonson may have written more in detraction than in truth: he did not care for this style of play), would have
been disguised as far as possible by music or by thunder—for also in the
hut was the cannon-ball which was rumbled down the thunder-run for this

[1] *The Court and the London Theatres during the Reign of Elizabeth* (1913).

purpose. The effect was also produced from up there by beating a drum. Lightning, shooting stars, and similar effects were contrived probably by means of fireworks running down from the Heavens on a fixed wire.

At this point it is necessary to pause briefly again, to answer an objection. Bernard Beckerman has stated[1] that 'about the machinery in the heavens the Globe plays offer no evidence whatsoever'; and he ends the passage in which he amplifies this assertion by saying that 'the history of flying apparatuses in the Elizabethan theatre needs further study. For the Globe, at least so far as the plays demonstrate, no machinery for flying existed.' Maybe; but two things work against this assertion. Firstly, whatever the now surviving plays may demonstrate, the engraved views of the Globe demonstrate a different thing. On all the pictures of the Globe, and in common with all other theatres (except the Hope, as mentioned above), is shown the hut structure over the stage. Indeed, at the Globe this is more pronounced than in any other playhouse. The First Globe (see Visscher's view, Plate 1) shows a very complex arrangement, and the rebuilt Second Globe (see Hollar's drawing, Plate 5) a very massive one. If these structures did not house the flying machinery, what could have been their purpose, situated where they were? Secondly, Dr. Beckerman, following a thorough, analytical computation, shows that during the ten-year period under his review no less than 150 new plays were presented at the Globe. Of these there have survived no more than twenty-nine. Yet it is upon the evidence of these twenty-nine only, discounting 121 others, that Dr. Beckerman makes his assertion. Now, Elizabethan plays survived when they were committed to print; that is, when they were deemed to have value as literature beyond the immediate purposes of the stage (thus, of the surviving Globe plays half are by Shakespeare). But these are the very sorts of plays which are least likely to be much concerned with flying machines and other fantasies of mechanical paraphernalia. Therefore if flying effects were allowed for at the Globe, as the over-stage huts suggest that they were, they would have been more likely to be used in the 121 lost or unpublished plays of Dr. Beckerman's calculation than in the surviving twenty-nine; and thus it remains reasonable to assume that flying machinery was housed in this position, even if, as may be, it was rarely used.

[1] *Shakespeare at the Globe, 1599–1609* (London, 1962).

But the term 'Heavens' need not have referred only to the hut and the roof. It is possible that there was some upper gallery, which cannot be seen in the Swan drawing because of the angle from which the sketch has been made, which also could have formed a part of the Heavens feature. Most commentators now agree on this. The only difficulty it raises is that of the actual height of the shadow-roof above the stage. The present tendency is to conclude that the underside of the roof would have been on a level with the eaves of the theatre building. This would allow better visibility of the stage from the top gallery of the auditorium, which, if the 'shadow' jutted forward from *below* the eaves level, as is shown in the Swan drawing, would have provided a rather impaired view on this account. However, if the 'shadow' were to be raised high up to the eaves-line, it would necessitate elongating, in what I think is a most improbable way, the two pillars supporting it in front. Clearly the two pillars in the Swan sketch are intended to be in the classical style and proportion. But to raise them in anything like classical proportion to the height of approximately 30 feet (which is what would be required) would be to make them unwieldily massive for their job. On the other hand, to make them of that height but slender, would be to add structural difficulties to architectural improbabilities; for two such tall, slender, single-piece shafts of timber would not only be unsuitable for carrying a permanent weight but, moreover, would not be easy to get. And even if, as Adams suggests, ships' masts could be satisfactorily used for the job, the result would still have been so out of character with the Elizabethan style and method of building that I, for one, think it more likely the pillars were kept pretty well within the classical proportion, that they therefore did not rise to the eaves-line, and that people in the top galleries whose view was consequently impaired by the 'shadow', were obliged to make the best of it, as we have to do today in some of the upper galleries of our own theatres. To this subject also we shall return at a later stage of our inquiry.

For the moment, then, there is no reason to disbelieve in the existence of a third storey in the tiring-house façade, and if it existed it would probably have embraced a part of the function of the Heavens. The zodiacal signs and stars that were painted upon the ceiling could have surrounded this also. There is in Webster's *The White Devil*, v. iv, a scene where

Flamineo is confronted by a ghost. Flamineo outfaces it, speaks boldly to it, asks where it comes from, whether from Heaven or Hell. The words had their familiar theatrical connotation. Hell was the place beneath the stage, out of which ghosts, devils, and infernal visions were wont to rise up through a trapdoor. It was the 'cellarage' in which the voice of Hamlet's dead father was heard. And Heaven as we have seen was the region over the top of the stage. So Flamineo puts his question to the ghost in a theatrical metaphor: 'In what place art thou?' he asks, 'in yon starry gallery, or in the cursed dungeon?'

From this we may assume there was a 'starry gallery' somewhere aloft, and it is reasonable to suppose it was in a third storey of the tiring-house façade. In my reconstruction sketch based on the Swan drawing (p. 150) I have contrived to keep a foot in both camps. I have kept the stage posts to a reasonable height (about 22 feet), have brought the 'shadow' down accordingly, and have tucked the starry gallery up inside it.

G. R. Kernodle considers that not all the scenes in which the gods appear on thrones in Elizabethan plays refer necessarily to the 'creaking' throne which descended, 'the boyes to please'. He quotes the displays of 'Thrones of Honour' used on occasions of royal or scholastic ceremonial to show how a god-like or allegorical tableau could be set high up in an ornamental façade. (Examples of this effect can be seen in Plate 35, where Peace sits throned aloft with War grovelling at her feet, or in Plate 37, where Peace and Plenty sit together presiding from their high throne over the Garden of Plenty.) John Cranford Adams considers that in *The Tempest*, III. iii, this high gallery was 'the top' where Prospero stood, invisible, to direct his Spirits at the magic banquet. But was this also 'the top' upon which Joan la Pucelle appeared in *1 Henry VI*, III. ii, *holding out a torch burning* to signal to her allies the way into the besieged town of Rouen? Both John Cranford Adams and Sir Edmund Chambers agree that it was. My only demur on the point is that the whole of the warfare which flounces back and forth and around the stage in this play is of such a pasteboard-and-trumpet kind that I cannot help but think the towns of Orleans and Rouen were in keeping, and may well have been represented in the simple terms of the *Laurentius* stage in Cologne (Plate 19). But that argument raises a subject beyond the scope of this chapter.

## 3. THE UNWORTHY SCAFFOLD

---

IN most of the attempts that have been made during the last sixty years
to establish a convincing reconstruction of the Elizabethan public playhouse, the main force of controversy has nearly always raged around that
area at the back of the stage which is sometimes called the 'tiring-house
façade'. In their various assessments of this feature most reconstructions
disagree with one another; yet, while students have been so earnestly con-
centrating upon this area of disagreement, they have accepted without
much question a number of preconceived opinions about the nature of the
great acting area, the stage itself. In estimating the character of the
Elizabethan theatre we are constantly being betrayed by the habits of our
modern theatrical experience. We try, seemingly in spite of better knowledge, to find some sort of a proscenium somewhere upon the Elizabethan
stage; to open up an 'inner stage', no matter how questionable the evidence
for its existence, and to thrust back into it a great portion of the action of

Elizabethan plays. In this way the tiring-house façade has, like a magnet, seemed to draw back both actors and students alike into itself, leaving the great stage in front of it empty and unattended. But let us change our point of view for a while; let us turn out backs upon the tiring-house, leaving its problems and disagreements still unresolved, and inspect some details of that feature which Shakespeare, in the Prologue to *Henry V*, called an 'unworthy scaffold'—the stage itself. There is reason to suppose that we have misinterpreted some of its features, which, if we can come to see them more clearly, may assist us when we return again to examine the tiring-house.

We cannot begin better than by re-examining the Swan drawing. We must try to bring to this not only the knowledge gained from all the research into theatrical history that has taken place since it was first discovered, but also, if we can, a 'fresh eye', as painters say, with which to try to see it as though for the first time. Looked at in this way it may seem to us that one of its most remarkable features is also one which has been so long accepted for a commonplace that it now passes as a thing not worth further inquiry. This is none other than that the drawing shows a large rectangular stage set out into a round arena, a square peg in a round hole. If we could come fresh to this arrangement, surely it would strike us at once as a rather clumsy and uncomfortable feature. Those two wedge-like spaces upon either side of the stage, how awkward they are, how offensive to the general sense of architectural fitness! One asks oneself, why did not the builders of the Swan carry the stage right across the yard from one side to the other? What is the purpose of those wedges? To accommodate the 'groundling' spectators in the yard? One supposes so, disregarding for the moment the well-known dandies sitting on the stage, who, in fact, would be likely to be sitting just here along the sides, blocking the view of those very groundlings. Surely this cannot have been a very advantageous place for groundlings to stand? Or let us look at this same feature at the Fortune. This, it will be recalled, was a square playhouse; here at least the square peg was fitted into a square hole, and, since we have the builder's contract for it, we can expect some very precise information as to how it was done. And yet here again the effect is most surprising. Here, by any logical interpretation of the contract, there is a space of ground running along each side of the stage between the stage and its neighbouring galleries, which, while it measured only 6 feet wide from stage to gallery, was no less than 27½ feet long. In other words, these two spaces, one on each side of the stage, have the dimensions of corridors or gangways rather than of convenient parts of the auditorium: and when we consider, as we shall do shortly, that the Elizabethan stage was probably built up much higher than modern stages are, so that spectators, to get a comfortable view, would be apt to stand a little way off, not close up against it, we are led again to think that, whatever their uses may have been, these spaces at the sides of the Fortune stage could hardly have been *designed* for the comfort and convenience of spectators.

The general feeling that these stage-side spaces are a piece of awkward-ness is reflected in the readiness of scholars to abandon them as untrue. On the face of it, it would seem to make a much better general design, as well for the round playhouses of the Bankside as for the square Fortune, if these stages were to taper, narrowing towards the front, thus opening out the side spaces and allowing better movement and more room for spec-tators in the yard. The *Roxana* and *Messallina* engravings (Plates 40 and 50) appear to give countenance to this notion, which has been adopted in a number of important reconstructions, the two most notable being Albright's in 1909, and Cranford Adams's in 1943. But still it will not do: it is not convincing enough. The combined evidence of the de Witt sketch and the Fortune contract alone, without counting any lesser arguments and deductions, is very strong, and the value of *Roxana* and *Messallina* is too unsure. We do not know what sort of stages, whether indoor or outdoor, permanent or temporary, public or private, these are meant to represent. We only know that in spite of their particular convenience in some respects, they are not typical of stages of the period as a whole. When the balance of the evidence is made and all the likelihoods assessed, one is left with the probability that the typical Elizabethan stage was rectangular, just as the Swan drawing shows it. In other words, we are left with an architectural design which, when set inside a round auditorium, we do not like very much, which we feel to be unsatisfactory, requiring some further explana-tion. It is a problem; and to attempt to alter it, to rectify the design to suit ourselves, to assume, for example, that the Swan drawing is inaccurate, and that it ought to have shown a tapering stage like the *Roxana* and *Messallina* ones—to assume such things as this simply to bring the drawing into line with our own ideas of architectural fitness, is to shirk the problem at just the point where, if we pursue it, if we press it hard where it appears so clumsy and inexplicable, we may prove to have hit upon the very root and spring of the matter, which will there open and reveal its explanation. For instance, the word 'design' has been used above: it was said that we feel something unsatisfactory about the *design* of the stage. And here we should pause, for surely in the modern sense there was no such thing as a *design* for an Elizabethan stage, nor yet for the playhouse it stood in. We have been betrayed by our modern approach. We should know well enough that these places were not designed on drawing-boards as they would be today, but erected according to rules of thumb and traditional methods by master masons and their craftsmen. We are not concerned here with designs, but with traditions. Is it not possible, therefore, that both the stage and the house it stood in were *traditional* in form, and that the only innovation made by James Burbage, when he erected the first public playhouse, the Theatre, in 1576, was to make a rough-and-ready combination of the two?

It has grown to be commonly accepted that the Elizabethan playhouse derived its form from that of the galleried inn-yards in which, in earlier days, the old stages were set up; and that the stage itself, being then an improvised affair, adopted certain of the features (doors, windows, galleries, and so on) which were found most useful and usual at those inns. This theory, for which there is no authentic evidence at all, has been given more credit than it deserves. Certainly it was common at one time for plays to be performed in inn-yards, but more than this we do not know, and we are not justified in assuming that the inn-yard gave any other feature to the theatres than the convenience of the use of galleries; a feature which could in any case have been seen already in use at the bull- and bear-baiting arenas on Bankside, years before the first theatres were built. In any case, the first theatres, as is generally agreed, were round or polygonal buildings, which does not argue very strongly for their resemblance to the yards of any known kind of inn. Surely the most apt question is: *what sort of a stage in fact was it that was set up, in the early days, in those inn-yards?* Are we perhaps justified in supposing that it was some traditional form of stage which was later transferred, perhaps with a few modifications, but substantially the same, to the round-shaped Theatre, then to the Curtain, and to all the other playhouses, of whatever shape, round, polygonal, or square, modifying, enlarging, aggrandizing itself perhaps in one way or another, but always remaining within touch of a tradition whose conventions were

Early amphitheatres on Bankside
(From Ralph Agas's map of London, published between 1560 and 1590)

fixed long before Burbage was a baby? There are things which lend some colour to this possibility. For instance, the Fortune builder's contract provides that this theatre shall be fitted with a stage 'contryved and fashioned like unto the Stadge of the saide Plaie howse called the Globe'. It seems to have bothered no one that the Globe was a round or polygonal building, while the Fortune was square. Evidently the character of the stage derived nothing from the roundness of the one or the squareness of the other, but had its own nature to keep to, and kept to it, no matter what the shape of its surroundings. Even when an improvised stage was set up indoors, where one might expect to find that it was built right across one end of a hall or room, one finds, instead, a stage built out from one wall into the middle of the room, just as the Swan stage was built out into the middle of the yard. Such at least is the stage we see in the well-known frontispiece to Kirkman's *The Wits; or, Sport Upon Sport*. It must surely be that one of the factors, probably the chief factor, maybe even the only factor which made this stage this shape, was the very strong factor of an abiding tradition.

Besides this it may be noted that contemporary visitors to the London playhouses appear to have been very impressed by them; but not for the technical reasons by which, if they had vouchsafed them, their descriptions could have been so useful to us today. What impressed them was simply the then very unusual business of providing a large, permanent, public auditorium; of the stages, and how plays were performed on them, and, for instance, whether there was such a thing as an inner stage or not, they have nothing whatever to say. One is tempted to think that in this regard they found nothing essentially different from traditional practices they had seen elsewhere, even in other countries, and so did not bother to report upon them.

The inferences, slender though they may seem, are worth pursuing, because we can at once point to the existence, in full flourish, of a traditional stage of the very type we are seeking. It is none other than the old street theatre, the booth stage of the market-place, the *théâtre de foire*. This is perhaps most familiar to us from engravings of seventeenth- and eighteenth-century strolling players, especially ·of the Commedia dell'Arte. But its lineage, as Richard Southern has pointed out,[1] is much older than that, and its descendants may still be found in modern times. Its earliest portraits are seen in Greek vase-paintings of popular comedies, while photographs taken not long ago at Tardets, in the Pyrenees (Plate 28), show Basque peasants performing their traditional folk-dances on this same traditional stage. The form has varied little from century to century. Basically it consists of no more than a platform supported on posts or trestles with, at the back of it, some sort of small house or tented enclosure, from which the actors come out. Here we may recognize, if we will, an early form of the Elizabethan tiring-house. The picture of this basic stage

[1] *The Open Stage* (London, 1953), pp. 15–16.

Frontispiece to *The Wits; or, Sport Upon Sport*
by Francis Kirkman, 1672

given on page 44 is general rather than particular: it purports to show a typical example of which all specific instances of which we have record are variants, in one degree or another. Perhaps as a modern reconstruction it is more elaborate and sophisticated than was common (though the example from Louvain in 1594, shown in Plate 23, is comparable in its ornament). The commonest type of stage in the sixteenth century was probably the one shown on page 33, as sketched from a painting attributable to Pieter Breughel the Younger or one of his followers. We see it again, a century later, in the engraved English title-page to Scarron's *Comical Romance* of 1676 (Plate 29). With some small additions it can quickly take on the more ornamental appearance of the Lyons *Terence* stages of the fifteenth century; or, elaborated almost out of recognition, but still fundamentally the same thing, it can present us with those baroque towers and arcades of the Flemish *Rederyker* stages of the sixteenth century which may be studied in Kernodle's *From Art to Theatre*. Here again we are on the threshold of the Elizabethan playhouse, as Kernodle shows.

But it may be thought desirable to find a more decisive reason to link these neighbouring but still foreign pieces of evidence with what we suppose to have been a similar practice in Elizabethan England. If so, a passage from Jonson's *The Poetaster* offers a clue. It must be remembered that this play is one of a group in which Jonson, Marston, Dekker, and, to a lesser degree, Shakespeare, were all involved in a curious, contentious affair, known as the War of the Theatres, which occurred between 1599 and 1602. Whether this dramaturgical row was concerned only with matters of literary taste between Jonson and Marston, or whether it reflected the rivalry between the public and private theatres at that time, is uncertain. What *is* certain, however, is that these plays were basically concerned with the literary and theatrical scene in London, that their references are all English, and that their speeches were addressed to English audiences who were assumed to be versed in the current affairs of the English theatre. Thus, in *The Poetaster*, III. i, we have the braggart Captain Tucca, a character somewhat resembling Pistol in his addiction to theatrical rodomontade, who is addressing an actor, Histrio. He finds Histrio in a down-at-heel condition, and bids him to go to a certain famous playwright, who will mend his fortunes for him. Says Tucca: 'Go, he pens high, lofty,

in a new stalking strain bigger than half the rhymers in the town again; he
was born to fill thy mouth. . . . If he pen for thee once, thou shalt not need
to travel with thy pumps full of gravel any more, after a blind jade and a
hamper, and stalk upon boards and barrel heads to an old crack'd trumpet.'
Here, then, is the picture, familiar to all that London audience, of the poor
English player, tramping from place to place, with stones in his shoes, and

Stage on barrel-heads: after a drawing by Pieter Breughel the Elder

acting his plays 'upon boards and barrel heads'. Now let us turn to the
sketch shown on this page. This is taken from a detail in a drawing attributed to Pieter Breughel the Elder. It is dated 1559. Here is a booth
stage, and here are the barrel-heads. Or, seeking further, we find the 1581
drawing of the *Laurentius* stage at Cologne (Plate 19). Here are not only
the barrel-heads but the boards as well, all clearly set out, almost for counting. What more is needed to show a definite link of common theatrical
practice between England and the Low Countries? If it does not satisfy
every critic (and admittedly it is still not absolute), it certainly satisfies me.

   There are two special characteristics of this traditional street theatre
which recur so frequently in pictures of it as to deserve our special attention.
One is that it seems not to have had any fundamental qualms about revealing the naked trestles that supported its stage. True, these were often

hidden behind draperies; but when, as often happened, they were allowed to show, this would seem not to have been necessarily from lack of means (for in the Lyons woodcuts illustrating Terence's *Andria*, which show a pleasantly ornamented stage façade, not lacking for the necessary decorative skill or expense, we find at the same time that the naked timbers

Booth stage: after a drawing by Pieter Breughel the Younger

beneath the stage are plainly represented), but simply, we must suppose, because an audience was willing, at need, to accept the convention of turning a blind eye upon things which did not come within the action of the play. When Shakespeare called his stage an 'unworthy scaffold' he was not using the word scaffold in any metaphorical sense. It was in his day an ordinary synonym for stage. A stage was simply a scaffold for actors, differing little from that other scaffold upon which, perhaps in the selfsame market-place, the public executioner performed his own mystery; and in both cases the scaffolding itself might be either draped or left bare as occasion dictated; and in neither case did it matter much, so long as the performers were raised up high enough for all the crowd to see them.

This brings us to the second characteristic feature we are to notice as having been typical of the street theatres; this is the unusual height of the stage, as compared with our modern custom. It varied, of course, and not every contemporary picture will support the claim; but the evidence is good and plentiful enough to show that the stage-floor of typical street theatre was set level with the tops of the heads of the spectators standing around it, if not a little higher (Plate 22). The reason for this is obvious. The shows were meant to be seen by large crowds standing on flat ground, and if the people at the back were to be able to see, then the spectacle had to be raised up high enough for them to do so: the only alternative would have been to have the spectators themselves raised on stands, or on a raked floor, which was here out of the question. This, as we know, was the case with the medieval street-shows, where the stages, either static or on wagons, were frequently set high enough to allow for a dressing-room underneath. One of the best pictures we have of the pageant cars of the old medieval tradition is 'The Triumph of Isabella', an early seventeenth-century Flemish painting now in the Victoria and Albert Museum. Two extracts from this are shown in Plates 30 and 31. The whole painting shows a procession of ten splendid cars, part of the celebrations in honour of the Archduchess Isabella of the Netherlands in 1615. The picture is skilfully and realistically painted, and from it we can judge that the floor-level of the various cars was set at about 5 feet 6 inches above the ground. Another picture, van der Meulen's painting in the Liechtenstein Gallery, Vienna, of a stage set up in a market-place, a very circumstantial and fully detailed record dating from the 1660s, gives a similar result—though here 5 feet 6 inches would appear to be the minimum height, and one might even put it a little higher (Plate 21). Several other pictures revealing this habit for stages to be high can be found among the plates at the end of this book. In general, a reasonable guess would put the normal stage height for a street theatre playing to standing spectators as somewhere between 5 feet 6 inches and 6 feet above ground.

These, then, are some of the characteristics of a traditional stage which I here suggest was the immediate parent of the Elizabethan one. We can imagine it, quite small at first, being erected in the yards of the London inns; then having room to expand in Burbage's newly built arena, enlarging itself and the little tabernacle at the back, the rudimentary tiring-house, enlarging itself also, adding an upper storey or even two, incorporating itself into the structure of the main building, and presently, with the further addition of a canopied Heavens, becoming the façade we know—or think we know. We must recall, however, that this is not the course of development that has hitherto been supposed; the theory has been that the features of the tiring-house were originally adapted from the existing gallery framework of the auditorium, and its general design was fundamentally conditioned by this framework. But it must be remembered that this is no more than a conjecture; there is no special evidence for it; and although the theory here offered as an alternative is also conjectural, there are a few indications of something which, if they are not evidence to support it, at least nod in that direction. For instance, it will be remembered that in the Fortune contract the builder is first given his instructions for building the playhouse 'frame', i.e. the general structure of the auditorium, and is then given further directions for a 'Stadge and Tyreinge howse to be made, erected & sett upp *within* the saide fframe'. The italics are mine, and I emphasize the word because it seems to indicate that not only the stage but the tiring-house also was thought of as a separate structure. Furthermore, it is quite clear in the Swan drawing that the tiring-house façade is flat and that it stands forward and apart from the round structure of the auditorium, in which it may be incorporated, but of which it is *not* an essential member.

However, it is not with the tiring-house but with the stage that we are at present concerned. We will assume, at least for the time being, that this theory as to the origin of the Elizabethan stage structure is correct. Approaching it from this angle, let us see what new light is thrown upon the business of reconstruction. First, let us go back to the street theatre where we left it just now, to consider again the height of the stage.

If it is agreed that, in the period we are studying, an outdoor stage for a standing audience would tend to be a high one, about level with the top of a man's head, may we not assume that this characteristic was continued

in at least some of the Shakespearian playhouses? There is a strong argument for this. We know that an indispensable feature of these theatres was
the space under the stage called the 'Hell', and to allow for this, most, if not
all, reconstructions hitherto (which provide for a stage between 4 and 5
feet high, and no higher) have had recourse to an excavated cellar beneath
the stage, to give the necessary headroom. This immediately raises a
problem, for the evidence of the Hope Theatre is certainly against it; here,
we are told, the stage was made 'to be carryed or taken awaie, and to
stande uppon tressels', so that when desired the arena could be left free
for 'the game of Beares and Bulls to be bayted in the same': which means
that in this case a dug cellar cannot be considered as at all probable. But,
in any case, to have gone digging cellars on the Bankside of Shakespeare's
day was to go digging for trouble. Whenever the Thames was at high tide
this locality was then little better than a marsh, and the rising water was
collected in ponds and ditches which, as the tide went down, discharged
it again into the river. The Globe playhouse itself was, as Ben Jonson tells
us, built upon piles, 'Flancked with a ditch, and forc'd out of a Marish'.
We can imagine, if we must, that the builders, being determined to provide
Burbage with a cellar, may have dug down 1 foot or, with some ingenuity
and a good deal of pumping, 2 feet. Deeper is unlikely: and in view of what
we have seen at the Hope, and of what we have seen of the street theatres,
is it not more likely that they dug no cellar at all, left their yard flat, and
built their stage up high, like other stages?

In a speculation like this where exact evidence is all too rare, we are often
obliged, for want of better, to accept the most reasonable probability, which
is in this case that a typical Elizabethan public theatre stage was apt to be
much higher than we have formerly imagined, and that the activities of
the Hell took place on a level with the groundling spectators around it,
in the same way that it had always happened in medieval times. The actor
had the heads of his groundlings not at his knees but at his feet, and Ben
Jonson's pun about the '*under*standing gentlemen o' the ground' gains
point when we see his speaker standing so high above them.

Turning now to the actual structure of these stages, we find that we
have evidence of four of them, and that these are all different. In three
of these cases the evidence is direct; in the fourth, the Globe, it is inferred.

First is the Swan, and our evidence is, of course, the drawing. It appears clear enough to be acceptable that the draughtsman intended to present what we will call an open stage, that is a stage left open beneath, so as to reveal its supports. We have already seen that this was not an unusual feature in the street theatres, and so its presence here at the Swan is no freak, but a direct link with tradition. We wish, however, that we could make more sense out of those two great baulks with which the front of the stage appears to be supported. Presumably there were two others farther back, beneath the two pillars supporting the Heavens, where they would certainly have been needed. A reconstruction along these lines would make sense, except that some sort of modification would be needed to provide support for the two forward corners of the stage. But these are details which tend to take us beyond the thread of our present study. Having found at the Swan some evidence for an open stage, we will pass on to the Fortune, where we can be certain of the opposite.

From the builder's contract we learn that the Fortune stage measured no less than 43 by 27½ feet, and since no other reference is given we must understand it to have been rectangular in plan. Its height above ground is not specified. However, we are told that it is to be 'paled in belowe with good stronge and sufficyent newe oken bourdes', and soon after there follows a further detail about this, which seems hitherto to have been misunderstood, to judge from previous reconstructions based upon the contract. The passage in question provides that 'all the princypall and maine postes of the saide fframe [i.e. of the house] and Stadge forwarde shalbe square and wroughte palaster-wise with carved proporcions called Satiers to be placed & sett on the topp of every of the same postes'. From this it must be assumed that the stage was all supported underneath with posts, of which those on the outer or 'forwarde' side were to be cut square, ornamented at the tops with the carved Satiers, and set 'palaster-wise' against the paling of oaken boards previously referred to. The effect thus produced is shown in the drawing at the opening of Chapter 2 (and it may be noticed in passing that it is not unlike the front of the stage in the well-known woodcut from Parabosco's *Il Pellegrino*). The significance of this is that the stage is *seen* to be carried on posts in the traditional manner. The paling appears only as a sort of curtain wall between the posts.

As was said above, however, other reconstructions have interpreted this passage differently. In these the 'princypall and maine postes of the . . . Stadge forwarde' have been judged to belong not to the stage proper but to the tiring-house façade, and there, 'palasterwise', some posts have been duly arranged. The point is important to us here, and in a further instance which will arise later, because it involves our interpretation of the word 'stage' as the Elizabethans understood it. In the modern sense it is an elastic word involving not only the boards and timbers of the stage itself, but, if need be, the whole area in which it is set, the atmosphere with which it is invested, and indeed the very profession of those who act upon it. Not so to the Elizabethans. To them a stage was a scaffold, a raised floor, and no more; and we ought not to interpret their use of the word in any wider sense. The tiring-house was an adjacent but separate thing, and did not come within the meaning of the word stage.

It is similarly interesting to note that our modern habit of referring to the Elizabethan form of stage as a 'platform stage' is equally out of keeping with their usage. For the Elizabethans the word 'platform' meant a groundplan, a levelled foundation, or even simply a design or policy, as we still do when we speak of a 'political platform'. A 'platform stage' would have been for an Elizabethan almost a contradiction in terms, and one does not find them using the expression. In Thomas Platter's account of his visit to a London playhouse in 1599 there is a sentence which Chambers (*Elizabethan Stage* (Oxford, 1923), Vol. II, p. 365) has translated as 'they play on a raised platform, and everyone can well see it all'. But Platter's actual words in the German are 'erhöchten brüge', which I take to mean a 'high-standing bridge-work'.

With all this in mind we will look at those parts of the Fortune contract which refer to the stage of the Globe. It will be remembered that the Fortune was built to rival the Globe, and the builder was directed to copy many of its arrangements. Certain differences are particularized, however. For instance, after the clause where it says that the Fortune stage was to be paled in below with oaken boards, it then goes on to say that it was to be 'in all *other* proporcions . . . contryved and fashioned like unto the Stadge of the saide Plaie howse called the Globe' (my italics). The word 'other' seems to imply the possibility that at the Globe the stage was *not* boarded in below, an implication which is later reinforced in a passage (already partly quoted above) which goes like this: 'To be made & doen to be in all other contrivitions, conveyances, fashions, thinge and thinges effected, finished and doen according to the manner and fashion of the said howse called the Globe *saveinge only* that all the princypall and maine postes of the saide fframe and Stadge forwarde shalbe square and wroughte palasterwise. . .' (my italics).

A stage supported on posts
Woodcut from Parabosco's *Il Pellegrino* (1552)

In other words, the principal and main posts of the stage at the Globe were *not* square as they were at the Fortune; therefore presumably they were round. And they were not set pilasterwise, as indeed, not being square, how could they have been? How, then, was the stage boarded in below? There are two possibilities: either the boards were set fully behind the outer posts in such a way as to leave them standing free, or else they were set fully in front of them, to make a continuous panelling in which the posts did not feature. Either is possible; but neither seems to be quite in tune with the likely practice of an Elizabethan joiner. At any rate we ought to consider a third possibility, which is that the stage was not boarded in at all, but was left open. 'They might distinctly perceive a goodly stage to be reared (shining to sight like the bright burnished gold) upon many a fair pillar of clearest crystal.' The passage in *The English Wagner Book* of 1594, from which that sentence is taken, is quoted by Chambers as aptly reflecting—though in glorified terms—the general effect of the Elizabethan public stage, and it begins by emphasizing those ranks of supporting pillars which, we suggest (allowing for some poetic licence in the matter of the clearest crystal), were a well-known stage feature.

And not only pillars but trestles. The last of the four stages in our evidence is that of the Hope, which as we have already noticed, was made to stand upon trestles 'to be carryed or taken awaie'. Here, if the stage was boarded in, there is nothing in the Hope contract to suggest it; the general structure of trestles does not offer any very suitable way of doing it; and the character of the thing, from a traditional point of view, is entirely against it. Probability here again inclines on the side of a stage open below.

Thus of our four stages only one is known for certain to have been paled in. With each of the others there is some reason to believe that the structure was an open one of posts or trestles, not concealed behind boards. But this is not to say that the structure was therefore left naked. Although we believe that in the street theatres this was sometimes done, and although we have the immediate evidence of the Swan drawing to the same effect, there is also some evidence which tells us that this was not the usual course. The stage was closed in below, not with boards but with hangings. This had been a practice with the street and booth stages from the very beginning, and its vestiges are hanging upon every Punch and Judy show to this day. For Elizabethan times, there is quite a lot of familiar textual evidence which will back up a theory that the Fortune stage, in being panelled, was not typical, but an innovation. The evidence for hangings has been misunderstood because, as stated above, scholars have allowed themselves to believe that the word 'stage' could be read as applying to the façade of the tiring-house. Thus when (in *The Rape of Lucrece*, l. 766) Shakespeare gives us:

Blacke stage for tragedies and murthers fell

we have been told that he meant not that the stage, the scaffold, was all hung round with black, like the scaffold for a public execution, but that some black draperies were used behind or over the stage. Indeed, this may also have been done, but first Shakespeare tells us that it was the *stage*, not the tiring-house, which was black. Again, in the Induction to the anonymous play, *A Warning for Fair Women*, we have the lines:

> The stage is hung with black, and I perceive
> The auditors prepar'd for tragedie.

Or there is the quotation from Sidney's *Arcadia*, describing the clouds coming over the sun, which 'blacked over all the face of heaven; preparing (as it were) a mournful stage for a Tragedie to be played on'. Note that the tragedy is played *on* the black and mournful stage, not 'within' or 'before' it. But if none of this is unambiguous enough, the following from Heywood's *Apology for Actors* leaves no doubt as to where the hangings were placed. He is speaking in the person of Melpomene and is purporting to describe the theatre of ancient time. His terms, however, as G. R. Kernodle says, are altogether those of a glorified Elizabethan stage, and in one sentence he refers to the matter of stage-hangings: 'Then did I tread on arras, cloth of tissue *hung round the fore-front of my stage*.' Taking this in conjunction with what we know of medieval practice, of the street theatres, of the stage-structures at the Swan and the Hope, and even possibly at the Globe, and remembering that Heywood's own theatrical connexion was with the Red Bull, so that he may have had that theatre most in mind when he wrote the passage given above, are we not justified in supposing that if there was ever such a thing as a 'typical' Elizabethan stage, we ought to imagine it as being hung all round with a great skirt of cloth, perhaps one of several sets of hangings of different colours suitable to different types of play, hangings which had been much used and roughly handled like the shabby splendours of some travelling circus today, and which sometimes hung loose so that the draughts would stir its fringes a little in the dust, or maybe sometimes were lashed tight from post to post, to keep the groundlings from peering in too much at the preparations being made for them in Hell?

Or sometimes these hangings would be pulled aside, and the occupants of Hell could run out with fireworks into the middle of the crowd. There is an episode in 'The Plot of the Play called England's Joy' which demonstrates this. 'The Plot', which is the only surviving example of an Elizabethan playbill, gives the outline of a spectacular play dealing, in the manner of an allegory, with the glorious victories of Elizabeth. It is entirely reminiscent of those animated triumphal arches and *tableaux vivants* erected for the state entry of James I into London, of the royal entertainments at Kenilworth and Elvetham, and of the mode of the Flemish *Rederyker* shows; and in keeping with all this it ends with an apotheosis and the display of a Throne of Honour. The Heavenly spectacle is then at once contrasted with a Hellish one. The whole sequence reads: 'And so with music both with voice and instruments she is taken up into Heaven, when presently appears a Throne of blessed souls, and beneath *under the stage* set forth with strange fireworks, divers black and damned souls, wonderfully described in their several torments' (my italics).

Now it can be objected that *England's Joy* is not in the first class of evidence, since so far as we know the play never existed. The existing *Plot* of it refers only to the hoax of March 1602, when one Richard Venner, having beguiled a large audience to the Swan to see this fabulous production, produced nothing, and welshed with the gate-money. *The Plot* is a dud prospectus; but as such it must have been written to be convincing to its readers, which it would not have been if it had promised an entertainment which, in the ordinary citizen's view, could not have been accomplished at the Swan. Besides, nothing in the whole document is foreign to what we already know of Elizabethan theatrical practice except this last item of a tableau presented under the stage. But may we not accept this also? It is already corroborated for us by de Witt that the Swan had an open stage. Thus the tableau described would have been presented between those two great supports under the stage shown in the drawing, and would surely have been revealed, when the time came, by drawing aside the stage-hangings.

But what of the visibility of this, when there was a mob of groundlings to shut out the sight of it from the galleries? What, then, was the visibility of similar devices in medieval practice? What problems were raised when the street performers of the Mysteries acted simultaneously between their pageant stages and the street (*Herod rages in the pageant and in the street also*, and *the 3 kings speaketh in the street* from the Coventry plays)? Presumably, as in the former time, the spectators would be kept away from that part of the ground needed in the action. A part of the yard could be roped off. Perhaps for a play like *England's Joy*, which had an unusually high entrance fee, there were no ground spectators at all, and whole portions of the play (there was to have been 'a great triumph made with fighting of twelve gentlemen at Barriers', as well as 'the battle at Sea in '88 with England's victory') might conceivably have taken place in the yard. In any case it need not be supposed that, necessarily, for all plays, the whole of the yard was always occupied by spectators. There is more than a little reason to believe that Elizabethan stage practice did occasionally include, if only for its novelty value, a certain amount of action in the yard. The possibility alone is enough to demand research. Is it possible, for example, that the barge in the last act of *Pericles*, in which Marina and her attendants were brought out to Pericles' black-sailed ship, was a practicable boat brought in through one of the gates of the yard and moored alongside the stage, which was the ship? Also there are a number of references, in early plays, to actors on horseback (*Enter a spruce Courtier a horsebacke*, from the anonymous play *1 Richard II*). Sir Edmund Chambers has suggested that this effect was simulated by the use of hobby-horses on the stage, but surely it is worth investigating the alternative, that there were occasions when real horses were ridden into the yard? It could so easily have been done.

But all this takes us beyond our present scope and plunges us perhaps too deeply into conjecture. We have here tried to show that the Shakespearian public stage had its origin in the common scaffold stage of the street theatres; that, like so many of these, it was built high, sometimes head-high to the spectators standing around it, always high enough to allow working space underneath without recourse to digging a cellar; and that it was usually an open structure of posts or trestles, draped round with hangings. We suggest that these conditions were general throughout Shakespeare's time, though with ever increasing degrees of modification (for example, it is probable that stages tended to become larger and more solidly built as the successful career of the public theatres went on), culminating in the large, fully panelled-in stage of the Fortune, which, I suggest, was in some respects ahead of its time. But in any case the old style was always just around the corner, and when the Hope was built, thirteen years after the Fortune and for the same proprietors, its stage was a trestled one in the oldest manner of all.

## 4. THE NATURE OF THE TIRING-HOUSE

THE tiring-house was that place at the rear of the stage in which the actors attired themselves (hence the name) and from which they came out into the action of the play. It corresponded in one sense to what we now call 'behind the scenes', but in another sense it was more than this: it was the scene itself. The word 'scene' has its origin in the Greek word *skene*, meaning a tent or booth, which was in fact, in the old Greek mime-theatre, that very same tent or booth behind the little portable stage whose persistence throughout theatrical history we have already noted. In the great classical theatres of Greece and Rome the word was maintained in its original sense, though by then it referred to large permanent buildings of wood or stone. The place which the Elizabethans called the tiring-house was, for the Romans, the scene; the monumental front wall of it facing the audience was the *frons scaenae*, or face of the scene; and the open area in front of this, on to which the actors came forth, was the *proscaenium*, that is, the place in front of the scene. Even as late as 1645 the word 'scene' was still understood in its primal sense. John Evelyn, visiting Rome and seeing the street actors there, writes in his journal: 'One thing is remarkable, their acting comedies on a stage placed on a cart, or *plaustrum*, where the scene or tiring-place is made of boughs in a rural manner, which they drive from streete to streete with a yoake or two of oxen, after the ancient guise.' The Elizabethans accepted this arrangement in its classical sense. Florio, in his *Dictionary* (1598), has: '*Scena*. The . . . forepart of a theatre where players make them ready, being trimmed with hangings'; and in the Swan drawing (whose declared purpose it is to point a similarity between the Elizabethan and the Classical theatre) the stage itself is correctly labelled 'Proscenium'. This original use and derivation of the scene-building or tiring-house is important to us because it is involved with the whole controversial subject of the 'inner stage', which we shall examine below.

We must note in passing that there is an instance of a 'tent' or 'tents' on the Elizabethan stage which may refer to the tiring-house in the sense of a 'scene', as given above. In September 1590 Thomas Platter visited the Curtain Theatre and saw a play in which the actors

represented various nations, with whom on each occasion an Englishman fought for his daughter, and overcame them all except the German, who won the daughter in fight. He then sat down with him, and gave him and his servant strong drink, so that they both got drunk, and the servant threw his shoe at his master's head and they both fell asleep. Meanwhile the Englishman went into the tent [*in die Zelten*], robbed the German of his gains, and thus outwitted the German also.

The question is, what was this tent? It might have been the tiring-house itself, hung all along with arras or curtains, thus still retaining something of the character of the original 'scene' or booth. On the other hand, Leslie Hotson has drawn attention to a passage in Jonson's *Poetaster*, which is related to this and provokes a different interpretation. In Act III, scene i, from which we have already quoted in the previous chapter, Captain Tucca is again addressing the actor Histrio. Tucca has heard that the actors are likely to impersonate him on the public stage. He threatens: 'An you stage me, stinkard, your mansions shall sweat for't, your tabernacles, varlets, your Globes and your Triumphs.' A tabernacle may be any sort of movable tent or booth; 'mansion', in theatrical history, was the medieval term for the demountable scenic house, or *locus*, used in the 'simultaneous setting' methods of the Mystery or Morality plays, a practice which certainly continued to a late date (cf. the stage for *Laurentius* at Cologne, Plate 19). Hotson effectively uses this quotation to show that such medieval practices were still common on the London public stage in 1601.[1] If he is right, as seems probable, then not only this reference but also the quotation from Platter, above, may belong more aptly to a later page, where the 'monument' in *Antony and Cleopatra*, and the 'pavilion' in *Pericles* are under discussion. Meanwhile, we are concerned with the body of the tiring-house itself.

Most reconstructors agree that the tiring-house was a portion of the main theatre building which had been divided off from the spectators and was used entirely for 'back-stage' purposes. Since the main building was round or polygonal, it followed that if the façade or 'scenic wall' of the tiring-house were nothing but a closed-off portion following the inner line of this, without addition, it would be, in plan, a shallow curve; or, more likely in a wooden building, three flat planes in shallow oblique. This arrangement has sometimes been adopted in reconstruction. The alternative is that the scenic wall was flat, either built a little forward of the main enclosing wall, or else as a chord between the two points of its inner circumference. I myself believe that the flat scenic wall is the more likely solution, since it has the authority of the Swan drawing and of classical practice, and since it accords better with the sequence of development which I suggest in the drawings in Appendix A. There is no essential logic in the belief, which has influenced most reconstructors, that, because the levels and dimensions of the main building were such and such, therefore the levels and dimensions of the tiring-house corresponded with them.

[1] *Shakespeare's Wooden O* (London, 1959), p. 68.

This may have been so; or it may partly have been so; but it is a characteristic of ordinary building in the Elizabethan period not so much to unify the whole as to build each unit for its own purpose, and then to close them all together in any convenient way. The dimensions of the main frame of the Fortune or the Globe do not necessarily govern the dimensions of their tiring-houses. The wording of both the Fortune and Hope contracts suggests that the tiring-houses were separately considered.

We have, then, a façade which we will assume to have been in a straight line, closing the back of the stage. We can suppose that it rose to something like the full height of the surrounding auditorium, that is of three storeys, comprising an average over-all height of about 30 feet. The openings in this façade, giving on to the stage, may have differed somewhat between one playhouse and another, but the conventional arrangement with which we are familiar is near enough to the style and requirements of the time to be accepted, at least as a starting point. According to this we have, on the stage level, a central opening closed in with arras or curtains, and two important doorways, one on either side of it; on the floor above this an open gallery flanked by two smaller openings or windows, sometimes represented in reconstruction as oriel or bay windows; and perhaps above this another storey, with window or gallery openings.

So far, so good. Now we have to examine a popular theory that the central opening on the stage level was an 'inner stage' which was capable of being opened and closed and was constantly used in support of the forward or main stage, and that the gallery above this was called the 'upper stage', having special uses of its own. For instance, John Cranford Adams, in his book *The Globe Playhouse, its Design and Equipment*, not only prescribes for these areas an extensive and particularized range of functions around which he claims the whole method of Elizabethan play-structure was composed, but gives exact measurements into the bargain. Yet this really goes far beyond the warrant of evidence. We know, certainly, that the Elizabethans used an area which they called the 'upper stage', and this we shall discuss shortly. But we do *not* know how or to what extent they recognized such a place as an 'inner stage'. The Swan drawing does not show such a thing, and the wording 'inner stage' does not occur anywhere in the whole corpus of Elizabethan theatrical literature (as indeed it could not, for according to the Elizabethan understanding of the word stage, such a phrase would be meaningless).[1] The nearest equivalent known to me is the one used in a stage direction by Greene in *Alphonsus of Arragon*: 'Let there be a Brazen Head set in the middle of *the place behind the stage*.' The italics are mine. I would draw attention to the fact that the occasional and auxiliary use, however often, of a place recognized as being *behind* but not *of* the stage proper, does not constitute an 'inner stage' in the sense of an alternative acting area for special purposes, such as to represent 'interior' scenes, which is the theory offered by Cranford Adams and others. The point is not a small one. It surely connotes a whole difference of character in theatrical presentation.

This is not, of course, to question that there was, connected with most if not all Elizabethan stages, a part of the rear wall which was either permanently hung with curtain or arras, or where a curtain or arras could be put up when required.[2] The device of a 'discovery', that is, the dramatic opening of curtains to show a specially arranged group or set-piece, is constant and common. The opening of the curtains to 'discover' the caskets in *The Merchant of Venice* is one example among many. Professor Thorndike, in his book *Shakespeare's Theatre*, lists 158 indisputable examples where an arrangement of curtains or arras is used in this or some similar way, and these are only a sample. Yet in none of his examples need we suppose that any important phase of action was sustained *behind* the curtain line. The curtains are used, as in the case of the caskets quoted above, to show some furnishing or tableau to the actors on the stage outside, or sometimes to house a large piece of furniture, such as a bed to which the actors retire— as in *Romeo and Juliet*, IV. iii, where Juliet *falls upon her bed within the curtains*. But if a bed is to feature in a more extended scene, then it is likely that

[1] Cf. p. 38, above.

[2] Since this was written it has been argued by Richard Hosley ('The Discovery Space in Shakespeare's Globe', *Shakespeare Survey 12*, pp. 42–43) that the stage hangings at the Swan were likely to have been hung along the whole length of the tiring-house below the gallery, hiding the doors, which would stand open behind, and leaving a little space between the hangings and the façade wall. This, he argues, would give the appearance shown in the *Roxana* and *Messallina* stage pictures (Plates 49, 50). A similar effect is also shown, though in a different context, in my sketch on page 91. Of course, no hangings at all are shown in the Swan drawing; but that some did exist there on at least one occasion is evidenced by a report that the angry crowd 'made great spoil' of them after the *England's Joy* hoax of 1602, as Hosley points out.

instead of being left in the place behind the stage it will be thrust forward on to it. Thus we find in Middleton's *A Chaste Maid in Cheapside* the direction: *A Bed Thrust out upon the stage; Allwit's wife in it*; and in Heywood's *The Golden Age* we have: *Enter the foure old Beldams, drawing out Danae's bed: she in it*, followed later in the scene by: *The bed is drawn in.* . . . These are only two of many examples of the thrusting in and out of beds upon the stage. It is clear from this and other instances that there was an established practice of bringing large properties forward on to the stage in preference to having a scene take place within a curtained recess. Even though it is possible to argue that there was no hard-and-fast standardization of method between one theatre and another or from one period to the next, it still seems to me a general rule that the action of a play, although it might look towards or enter from the tableau or set piece revealed by the opening of the curtains, would not usually take place within the recess. If this is so, it follows that the recess need not necessarily be very wide or deep. This is exemplified by the fact that in every case where actors do in fact enter the recess for some stated requirement of the play, it is always understood as representing a small, enclosed, or withdrawn place—a cell, a study, a cave, or a curtained bed.

The exaggeration of the importance, and also of the size, of the so-called inner stage in many reconstructions has perhaps been due to an erroneous theory that the inner stage was the embryo of our modern proscenium stage. According to this belief, as time went on the 'inner stage' was found to have a greater and greater value in performance, so that the Elizabethan actor came to centre more and more of his action in and around it. It has been supposed that 'interior' scenes were acted in it throughout, that it began to be used not only for set pieces but for furnished 'settings', that its size was increased until, at the Restoration, its outer frame had enveloped nearly all the original open stage and had become the 'proscenium arch' of today. The facts do not bear out this theory. Movable scenery, which gave rise to the proscenium arch, was not *developed* as an aid to drama upon the public stage, but was *invented*, complete, as an ingenious toy for the entertainment of the Court. When during the Restoration this invention was married to the public London theatres, the actors still did not perform in the midst of it, as they do today, but well out in front of it, upon the large apron stage which was the descendant of the open stage of Elizabethan times. The proscenium arch did then develop, but *not* by an enlargement of a former 'inner stage'. The development has been well described by Richard Southern in his book *The Open Stage*, and I cannot do better than quote him here in full. We have already seen that the true 'proscenium' was the acting-place in front of the scene-building or tiring-house. Southern now continues:

When, after the Elizabethan period, Davenant produced his new form of Restoration stage and theatre, he desired to add movable scenery at the back, worked by machinery. Such an introduction would normally have covered up the doors of entrance and the balconies which were formerly in the tiring-house wall—and their loss could not be tolerated since they formed an essential part of contemporary dramatic technique. Further, the new scenery demanded some sort of 'frontispiece' to frame it and to mask the machinery which worked it.

But Davenant's stage was built in a narrow hall instead of a wide polygonal ring, such as was the Elizabethan play-house, and so it presumably had to spread right across the building. That is to say the *proscaenium* (or stage) now reached to the side walls of the house. In these side walls . . . the essential doors and balconies could now be built . . . thus giving access upon the *proscaenium* but from the sides instead of the back (which was thus left unused and free for scenery).

What more logical than that the doors which gave upon the proscenium should be called the proscenium doors, and the walls which flanked the sides of the proscenium and held those doors should be called the proscenium sides, and that the ceiling joining the unity above should come to be called the proscenium ceiling, or top?

Thence it is an easy step to call the whole unity . . . the 'proscenium', with that shortening of phrase which is so often met in the speech of a craft or profession. Any other attempt to trace the origin of our proscenium is, I think, ill-founded.

We have already noted that the term 'inner stage' does not occur in Elizabethan texts; when, however, we come to consider the 'upper stage', we find a different case. The Elizabethans did occasionally use the term. In Day's *Humour Out of Breath* we come across the stage direction: *Re-enter Florimel and Assistance on the upper stage*, followed a little later by the direction that a game of blind man's buff, from which two other characters below had been resting, *is renewed on the lower stage*. One of many familiar examples embodying the use of the upper level occurs in *The Merchant of Venice*, II. v, where: *Enter Jessica, above, in boy's clothes.* She speaks with Lorenzo who awaits her below, throws him down a casket, then: *Exit above*, then, seven lines further on: *Enter Jessica below.*

The frequent dramatic use of what seems to have been a permanent upper level is the most characteristic single feature of Elizabethan stage practice. That this may even have been derived from a common practice in the old booth theatres is indicated by the frequent appearance, in contemporary pictures of these, of a ladder within the booth, poking over the top of it, on which characters can mount to an 'above' position (cf. pp. 32, 33). Developing from this, one is surely not being fanciful in pointing out that the business of vertical display, of building, mounting, and climbing upwards, seems to have had a characteristic and symbolic importance in the Renaissance theatre as a whole. In its pageantry the use of artificial hills and mountains (as for example the favourite 'Parnassus' device, a tall 'rock' on which costumed musicians were seated, with 'Apollo' on the summit) or the placing of actors on the eminence of high triumphal arches or façades were all well-known theatrical spectacular effects. The provision of some sort of practicable high place was therefore an essential ingredient of the Elizabethan theatrical scene.

The commonest and simplest form of it is that quoted above: one character watches, or speaks down to another character below, as from the balcony or window of a house, e.g. Juliet at her window, with Romeo below. Another common form, especially in the earlier plays of the period, is the use of the upper level as a podium from which an introductory character may comment upon the unfolding of the play below. Thus in Greene and Lodge's *Looking Glass for London & England* the prophet Oseas sits throughout the play on an upper level, to which he is brought in by an angel, and from which he makes moral comments during the intervals. In Marston's *Antonio's Revenge* the ghost of Andrugio watches from above the working out of vengeance for his own death. That is simple enough. But then we turn to *The Taming of the Shrew*, and find that not only is the upper level the place from which Christopher Sly and his 'wife' sit to watch the whole play, making comments from time to time ('would 'twere done!') but also that the whole previous introductory scene of Sly's awakening in the lord's bedroom, nearly 150 lines of good comedy, takes place 'aloft'.

That means that the upper level is here required to house a bed, some chairs, six actors with speaking parts, and one or two attendants. What sort of an upper level is this, in which such a scene can be effectively played to a large audience?

The upper stage is usually represented in reconstructions as a balustraded open gallery, continuing the line of the auditorium galleries on the middle level. Such an arrangement is well suited to simple house-and-window scenes, as those from *The Merchant of Venice* and *Romeo and Juliet* quoted above; but it surely presents difficulties when it has to cope with this scene from *The Taming of the Shrew*. I cannot feel convinced that any sustained scene can be theatrically effective if the audience has to watch it through the bars of a railing, set back as it were in the first-floor opening of a wall, especially when there is a large stage standing idle and empty below it between the spectators and the play. Yet there is a strong theory, supported by Chambers and championed to the utterance by Cranford Adams, that the upper level was always used to represent bedchamber and upper-room scenes. Adams, for instance, would have us believe that the whole of the great scene between Hamlet and his mother, with the killing of Polonius (*Hamlet*, III. iv), was written to be played in this situation. True, in Adams's reconstruction his upper stage is very large and visible, and he takes care to space the individual balusters of his railing very wide. Yet, still, a theory which ascribes to the Elizabethans such a hard-and-fast literal localization (upstairs rooms must be seen to be up, and downstairs rooms seen to be down) strikes me as foreign to the general character of their drama, and I cannot personally believe that any such scene as that just quoted from *Hamlet* can have been acted anywhere but out on the main stage.

None the less, Adams might justly point out, and I would have to agree, that whatever may have been done in *Hamlet*, the text of *The Taming of the Shrew* clearly requires us to accept an upper stage capable of sustaining the comedy scene described. Nor is this a solitary example. Most of the first Act of *Titus Andronicus* was written to be played on two levels. The upper one is designated as 'the Senate House' and once as 'the Capitol', and the play opens with 'Tribunes and Senators' entering and taking their places there. Later they are joined by three other characters, and we may suppose that there must be about ten persons, perhaps more (depending upon the number of senators) ranged ceremonially on their seats in this 'Senate House'. There is a deal of speech between the dignified senators above and the warring factions below. Characters come and go between the two levels, though the communicating stairs would seem to be out of sight of the audience, probably within the tiring-house, because one character, before ascending, says, 'Open the Gates and let me in', and then there is a flourish of trumpets and *They go up into the Senate House.* Later there is *a long Flourish till they come down.* A sketch of this whole scene is given at Plate 73, as part of a conjectural series on tiring-house developments, and the matter is further discussed in the related Notes. In another play, Lodge's *Wounds of the Civil War*, a similar arrangement is indicated. Here the place is throughout called 'the Capitol'. As before, in *Titus Andronicus*, the play opens with a ceremonial entry of dignitaries 'on the Capitol', and there is speech between those on the Capitol and those on the stage below. There is a Throne of State on the upper level, and the warring factions of Scilla and Marius contend for this throughout the play. As before, there is some coming and going between the two levels, and it seems that in this case the ascent to the upper stage may have been visible to the audience, since at one point Scilla's party *brave the Capitol*, and at another a stage direction tells us that *Cinna presseth up* to it.

It is interesting to note regarding these three plays, *Titus*, *The Shrew*, and *The Wounds of the Civil War*, that all three are circumstantially connected. All were first published and acted between about 1590 and 1594, and all were played either by Philip Henslowe's company (the Admiral's Men) or in one of his theatres within this brief period. The theatre in question may have been the one at Newington Butts, and here certainly for a short while in 1594 the Admiral's Men and the Chamberlain's Men gave a joint season of plays which included not only *Titus Andronicus* and *The Taming of the Shrew*, but also Marlowe's *Jew of Malta*; and it is notable that the latter play contains an important use of the upper and lower stages (Barabas's device of the trapdoor with the cauldron beneath it, into which he falls). So it is possible that the facilities of a specially extensive upper stage existed at Newington Butts. This was an early theatre, and maybe the employment of the upper stage did not everywhere continue in this enlarged form; though that it did continue in a form not unlike it must be allowed, when we consider, as we now must, the final scenes of *Antony and Cleopatra*. This is generally ascribed to the years 1606–8. Here, it will be recalled, at the climax of the play, an upper level in the acting area is supposed to be a 'monument'. Upon this there has to be room for Cleopatra, Charmian, Iras, and two or more maids. There must be space for these to haul up the dying Antony, and to lay him, presumably with good visibility for the audience, before Cleopatra; and the place should presumably be suitable for staging the whole drama and poetry of their last parting.

It is evident at once that here there can be no balustrade, since this would gravely obstruct not only the visibility of the scene of Antony's death but also the mechanical business of heaving him aloft. Since contemporary pictures of upper stages without balustrades are available (Plates 27, 32) and although it is true these do not refer specifically to the English theatre, this may be accepted at once. But there is also the question of the height of the monument level above the stage. Antony has to be hauled over the edge on to the upper level by a small number of boy actors. The position for hauling is awkward. Adams suggests it was done with the aid of a pulley and ropes from above. I think rather that it was done with the sole aid of the men actors on the stage below, and that the haul was not much, if any, higher than these could reach—say between 7 and 8 feet. Was this, then, the height of the permanent upper stage?

Not necessarily: we have to consider that there may have been some impermanent special structure erected to serve as a monument. Let me conjecture how this might be done.

The conditions I wish to fulfil are, first, to have this scene not too far back from the audience: thus I would like to bring the monument structure somewhat forward from the tiring-house wall. Second, Cleopatra and her maids must be able to enter and leave the monument while still remaining on an upper level. Third, they must have a fair amount of room. Fourth, they must not be beyond the reach of the men on the lower stage. And fifth, their position must make some sense out of the following curious passage in the text: in Act IV, scene xv, Cleopatra, having just entered on to the monument, is approached by Diomedes, below. She speaks down to him, concerning Antony:

> How now! Is he dead?
>
> DIOMEDES. His death's upon him, but not dead.
> Look out o' the other side your monument;
> His guard have brought him thither.
> [*Enter, below,* ANTONY, *borne by the Guard.*]

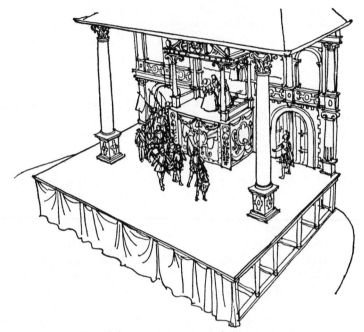

Cleopatra's monument. *Antony and Cleopatra,* IV. xv

Thus we find that Cleopatra is to look out first on one side of the monument, to speak to Diomedes, and then on the other, to see Antony carried in.

The sketch above fulfils all these requirements in a manner which I think simple and consistent with Elizabethan ideas. A small temporary upper stage has been built against the tiring-house façade, in front of the stage gallery, which here has no balustrade. It juts out on to the stage between the two main tiring-house doors, so that Diomedes, entering at one door, indicates that Antony is being carried in at the other, 'o' the other side your monument'. At the end of the scene the women bear Antony's body away through the gallery at the back. There follows one scene in Caesar's camp, and thereafter the play returns to end in the monument. I must say that I do not think that this final scene was actually played *upon* the monument in the same way as before, but rather that most of it, if not all, took place on the main stage, the monument being understood. If it were done 'aloft', however (which the text does not indicate), the arrangement described would still serve best.

This small temporary structure which we have just used for a monument is worth consideration in other ways. If hung with curtains it could serve well for many of the purposes which have usually been ascribed to the 'inner stage'. It would thus bring those necessary effects which are usually thrust back into 'the place behind the stage' forward and on to it, into the midst of the action. For instance, in *Pericles*, v. i, the scene opens on board Pericles' ship, off Mytilene. We have already been told by Gower, the Chorus of the play, that the stage itself represents the ship, and from the action it is clear that the silent figure of Pericles, mourning in sackcloth with long, unkempt hair and beard is revealed to the audience by the drawing of a curtain. The stage directions that put him in 'a pavilion on deck' are not in the original Quartos, but the action at the meeting of Pericles and his long-lost daughter calls for at least a fairly forward position; and so the structure that has served for Cleopatra's monument could serve again here, with a curtain before it, for Pericles' supposed 'pavilion'. Or, on other occasions, wreathed with greenery, it could become that favourite Elizabethan stage property, an arbour, such as that arbour in which Benedick hides himself and overhears the talk of Beatrice's love for him (*Much Ado About Nothing*, II. iii). Such a structure, if it were commonly used, might help to explain why no permanently curtained 'inner stage' is shown in the Swan drawing.

My argument for suggesting that such a fit-up structure was used has been so far only that it would have helped to bring the business of the rear alcove and of the upper stage forward into the principal acting area. On this alone I might have thought twice about suggesting it, were it not for two things. First, I find that Professor G. F. Reynolds, after a close analysis

in his book *The Staging of Elizabethan Plays at the Red Bull Theatre*, has come
to a similar conclusion, and gives many examples of the textual and
theatrical aptness of such a fit-up. Sir Edmund Chambers, too, is prepared
to accept it, speaking of the possibility of 'some porch-like projection from
the back wall' which may have been supported by posts; and Cranford
Adams has conjectured such a feature as being an intermediate development in the structure of playhouses. For the second argument, it is necessary to consider again what sort of curtained space for hidings and
discoveries there could have been on these Elizabethan stages, if no such
booth-like projection were used. Commonly, reconstructors have supposed an alcove or a recess, closed across with a curtain, under the first-
floor gallery, between the two flanking doors of the de Witt drawing. It is
perhaps the most convenient general answer, and I myself will be discovered making use of it, in Chapter 6 below. But of course de Witt shows
no such thing, and Richard Hosley has offered good argument[1] for be-
lieving that de Witt may be trusted in this as in other things. Moreover,
I have to admit that it sometimes seems to me there is something wrong
with the assembly of a façade which is closed fast at each side by two great
solid double doors, yet cannot be closed in the middle by more than
curtains. True, we may be dealing only with theatrical convention, and the
tiring-house is not necessarily here to be made weather-proof. True again,
there is occasional, but firm, evidence for some central place of entrance
in certain public-stage plays. But this could be answered by supposing a
third, central door. Though de Witt does not show such a thing, the idea
is strongly supported by an engraving of an imaginary 'Theatre', first
published in 1619 and recently brought to notice by Richard Bernheimer.[2]
The picture is shown here in Plate 18, and further discussed in the Notes.
If, then, the stage were backed in this way by a solid wall pierced with
three doors, the discovery space (or spaces) would be likely to have been
arranged in one of two ways: either by a continuous hanging a little forward
of the wall, with the doors hidden behind it (as Hosley suggests),[3] or by

[1] 'The Discovery Space in Shakespeare's Globe.'
[2] 'Another Globe Theater', *Shakespeare Quarterly*, Winter 1958.
[3] He also suggests that 'discoveries' could have been effected within the door openings themselves.
I am subjectively less satisfied with this idea than with the other.

a curtained, porch-like booth, set between the outer doors, as I have offered here.

One further thought on the question of the projecting alcove may now be given, before we turn elsewhere. If the proposition made in the previous chapter can be accepted, i.e. that the Elizabethan public stage was developed from the booth or street theatres, then in the course of that development there could well have been a time when the curtained booth, once the tiring-house itself, would have stood on the enlarged new stage of the permanent theatre, and up against the wall of the permanent tiring-house, with just the appearance of the little pavilion I have described. Being no longer necessary as a tiring-house, it might now have been dismantled, but since it was a part of the actor's traditional equipment, and likely to be used again whenever the company went out into the provinces, it would be kept handy in the store-room.

The growth of the stage and tiring-house of an Elizabethan public theatre along these lines is sketched in Appendix A. I do not, of course, pretend that these drawings are anything more than conjectural, but I believe that the truth lies somewhere within the field which they cover.

It will now be of interest to return to a problem of the upper stage which emerged briefly, above, in connexion with *The Wounds of the Civil War*: the possibility of a visible ascent from the lower to the upper stage. This is a matter which usually causes controversy among students of the subject —largely, perhaps, because it will not fit conveniently into any hard-and-fast scheme of reconstruction. There is in Middleton's *Family of Love* a remark by one of the characters who says that he went to a play at the Fortune, where he 'saw Sampson bear the town-gates [of Gaza] on his neck from the lower to the upper stage'. W. J. Lawrence quotes this among other examples which give him to think that there must have been some sort of staircase connecting the lower to the upper stage, in full view of the audience. Among other instances he gives the scene in *Julius Caesar*, V. iii, where Pindarus mounts a 'hill' to spy out the battle for Cassius, and then descends at his request to kill him. Cranford Adams refutes this latter example, but the former stands. I would add to it another, which occurs in *The Plot of the Play called England's Joy*, already referred to in Chapter 3. Here, in the second incident of the action, Queen Elizabeth enters and takes her throne, which is 'attended with Peace, Plenty, and Civil Policy; a sacred prelate standing at her right hand, betokening the serenity of the Gospel; at her left hand Justice; and at her feet War, with a scarlet robe of peace upon his armour; a wreath of bays about his temples, and branch of palm in his hand'. Here, in fact, is a tableau which students of the Renaissance theatre will recognize at once as a 'Throne of Honour'. It accords (as indeed does the whole description of the play) with the full formal and allegorical method of presentation made familiar by contemporary paintings and engravings, and which has been studied at length by G. R. Kernodle in his important book *From Art to Theatre*. An actual example from the London of 1604—only two years after the business of *England's Joy*—can be seen in Plate 36, where the central tableau under the title 'Londinium' represents the Throne of Monarchia Britannica, supported on either side by the virtues of Gladness, Veneration, Vigilance, Unanimity, and the rest. At her feet, where War had been in *England's Joy*, sits in this instance Divine Wisdom. There is nothing at first to suggest in the *England's Joy* text that the throne was supposed to be raised up like this, though from study of other instances one might already take it for granted. But then in the fourth episode there enters a cruel Tyrant (Spain) who mangles and wounds a beautiful Lady (Belgia) 'and so leaves her bloody, with her hair about her shoulders, lying upon the ground. To her come certain gentlemen, who seeing her piteous despoilment, turn to the Throne of England, *from whence one descendeth*, taketh up the Lady, wipeth her eyes, bindeth up her wounds. . . .' It does not, of course, follow that this throne would have been presented on the upper stage. I only offer the suggestion, since it suggests itself so strongly to me that such a throne could have been set upon the top of a rostrum like that discussed above for Cleopatra's monument, with an ascent arranged on either side as in the triumphal archway in Plate 36. It would thus be not only in the full Elizabethan style but far less extravagant than the 'high throne, wherein the King should sit . . . proudly placed with two and twenty degrees to the top'[1] which Chambers accepts as typical, in spirit at least, of the Elizabethan stage. Similarly, in Dekker's *Old Fortunatus* there is a dream scene where Fortune ascends to her throne: *Fortune takes her Chair, the Kings lying at her feet, she treading on*

[1] From *The English Wagner Book* (1594).

*them as she goes up.* And presently: *She comes down.* Again, in *Richard III*, IV.
ii, King Richard enters in pomp, and bids Buckingham:

> Give me thy hand. [*Here he ascendeth the throne.*]
> Thus high, by thy advice
> And thy assistance is King Richard seated . . .

How high was this? Was it high in metaphor only? It suggests to me that
an upper stage may have been used for this, and perhaps in other formal
throne scenes, with steps approaching it from the lower one.

But what, then, was the usual height of the upper stage? I have already
questioned whether the lower-stage alcove need have been so wide as it is
often represented. It is also possible that the upper stage was not raised so
high. Twelve feet is frequently suggested, since that is the height of the
corresponding gallery section of the auditorium, according to the Fortune
and Hope contracts. Yet if it is also true that the upper stage was used to
represent city or castle walls, as all commentators think they were, what
are we to suppose in those case where actors leap over or off these 'walls'?
Twelve feet is a considerable drop. I cannot feel it likely that the boy who
played Arthur in *King John*, IV, iii, when he had to leap down, was expected to leap from such a height, even with a heap of rushes or some such
thing to break his fall. It is true he has to be supposed as jumping from a
precipitous height, and that he kills himself by it, but since all this was
conveyed to the audience by conventional and not literal means, the
convention would hold equally well for a lower jump, perhaps between
7 and 8 feet.

The extent to which purely conventional practices were used on the
Elizabethan stage is not possible to determine, but we know for certain
that they were used very widely, and we are more likely to be right, when
faced with a puzzling stage situation, if we assume that it was disposed of
by some convention of even nursery-like simplicity, rather than by some
elaboration of theatre building which would have given a greater physical
realism to the scene. We know that some Elizabethan plays were conducted
according to the medieval system of 'houses', thrones, and other set pieces
standing simultaneously on the stage throughout the whole performance,
as shown in Plate 19. This is more characteristic of the earlier groups of

plays than of the Jacobean ones, though Reynolds demonstrates a probability that such methods were still used at the Red Bull as late as the
second decade of the seventeenth century. We have therefore to allow for a
possibility that these city and castle 'walls' may sometimes have been
pieces of practicable scenery placed on the stage; yet it still remains possible that in most instances the ordinary upper stage was used, and that in
the case of the *King John* scene of Arthur's leap it was not likely to have
been very high. This fits also with the requirement, noted above, for Cleopatra's monument to be within reasonable handing-up reach of those on
the stage below.

For dramatic purposes a conventional simplification may sometimes be
used even at the expense of the literal meaning of the text. In Jonson's
*The Devil Is An Ass* there is a scene (Act II, scene ii) between Wittipol and
Mistress Fitzdottrel which is supposed to take place as if at the upper
windows of two neighbouring houses. If one were to interpret the original
staging of this scene from the context of the spoken words only (to say
nothing of the stage direction: *Mrs. Fitzdottrel appears at a window of her
house fronting that of Manly's Chambers*), one would have no choice but to
suppose that these windows faced one another, as if across a street, and it
seems evident that that is what was in Jonson's mind when he was writing
the play. In the 1632 edition of the text, however, Jonson tells us in the
margin how the scene was actually done at the Blackfriars. It was 'acted
at two windo's, as out of two contiguous buildings', and so very contiguous
are they that we find as the scene proceeds that Wittipol *grows more familiar
in his Courtship, playes with her paps, kisseth her hands, etc.* Clearly it was theatrically more effective to play the scene like this, rather than to have the
characters framed in their windows at some distance from one another for
the whole length of the scene.[1]

The clear information we derive from this scene, therefore, is as follows.
It was played by adopting a convention which was presumably acceptable
to both audience and author, even though it did to some extent contradict
the text. The scene was 150 lines long, as long, that is, as the upper-stage
scene from *The Taming of the Shrew* which we have been considering above.
Four characters appear at the windows at one time and another, two in each.

[1] See also Plate 71, and related Note.

One wonders, then, how these windows were arranged at the Blackfriars. Presumably, in order to be seen from, and to have command of, all parts of the house, they would have been centred in the rear wall of the stage, like the windows in the *Roxana* engraving (Plate 50). In this case the actors would have been visible only from the waist upwards. We can accept this if we must, although it would have been hampering for the actors. There is, however, an alternative solution which suggests itself to me from a remark made by Mistress Fitzdottrel referring to these windows during a previous scene. She speaks of 'the Gentleman's chamber-window in Lincoln's Inn there, that opens to my gallery'. What *gallery* is she referring to ? Is it not possible that there was a small balcony with a railing round it in front of each window; or, come to that, one balcony running across the front of the two windows merely divided off in the middle; so that the characters coming out from each window could conveniently look into each other's houses or embrace each other, as required by the text? If so, we are back again at our little porch or booth. The engraving reproduced in Plate 54 of the Schouwburg in Amsterdam, although of a later date (1658), shows a small, central, porch-like upper stage of this kind in an indoor theatre.

Whichever way this window scene was done, however, it is clear that it was done in a fairly confined space. So perhaps after all the same condition could have applied to the bed-chamber scene of the awakening of Sly in *The Taming of the Shrew*; perhaps after all we do not need so much space and furnishing as we had at first supposed. *The Shrew* was also acted here, at this same Blackfriars, under the same windows, with perhaps that same gallery which exposed Mistress Fitzdottrel's adventure. And if it did not need much space at the Blackfriars, it can hardly have needed much more over the river at the Globe, or at Newington Butts (it was a popular play, much transferred from house to house). The play itself derives from the style of the Italian Comedians, whose typical acting background was, once again, the familiar booth stage of the fairs. So once again I will allow my-self to imagine the porch-like booth hung with its arras, standing between the two tiring-house doors. It backs up to the gallery floor, where, behind closed curtains, Sly lies snoring. A light stairway leads up on one side, and mounting this from below come the servants with apparel, basin, and ewer. They are now standing on top of the porch-booth in front of the curtain which represents the bed. They draw the curtain. Sly emerges. 'For God's sake,' he groans, 'a pot of small ale.' And so it begins. I cannot make up my mind, though, whether there would have been a railing or not.

While I am engaged in this conjecture I will add a footnote to it. Ben Jonson as a playwright is notable among his contemporaries as an innovator of stage technique. His deliberate method was to use his stage as a physical unity and to base his plays upon an acceptance of the fabric as it stood, as he did in *The Alchemist*, which is a unique example for its time of a play written entirely in and around one supposed house. Now, bearing this in mind, it is interesting to consider the following facts about *Bartholomew Fair*. The play was produced at the Hope. We know that the Hope had a movable stage on trestles, in the manner of the street theatres. Theatres of this type were also commonly seen at fairs; they were, as we have seen, little trestled stages with booths at the back of them. And it is a fact that in *Bartholomew Fair* the whole of the play, after the first scene, takes place *at* the fair, and upon a trestled stage, which, as the text makes absolutely clear, was for this presentation backed by something resembling a row of booths. I suggest that Ben Jonson was suiting his play to his theatre, and that it was his intention to use the fair-booth structure of the stage, as it stood, to assist the atmosphere of his play.

Tomb  Arbour  Throne  City Walls  and Gates  Green bank

## 5. THE STATELY-FURNISHED SCENE

THE criticism by Richard Flecknoe, in Restoration days, about the 'plain and simple' methods of Shakespeare's theatre, as having no scenery 'nor Decorations of the Stage, but onely old Tapestry and the Stage strewed with Rushes', has been more often quoted and had a much wider effect than the somewhat contradictory statement with which he followed it: 'For Scenes and Machines they are no new invention, our Masks and some of our Playes in former times (though not so ordinary) having had as good or rather better than we have now.' In Victorian times the 'plain and simple' view went unchallenged, though with it there went a puritanical approval of plainness and simplicity. The anonymous author of a popular educational work, *Old England*, published about 1857, may be taken as typical. He writes of the fire which ended the career of the First Globe,

a fire which, as is known, was started by some burning material from a
theatre cannon which was shot accidentally into the thatched roof.

The clumsy management of the cannons [says the writer] and the *thatched* theatre,
shows how comparatively unfamiliar were those who first witnessed the representation
of the most wonderful series of plays the world has seen, with those costly and laboured
contrivances to which in our day the soul of the art has been sacrificed. Poetry, wit,
passion, humour, wisdom, could be relished by our ancestors without them. . . . One
illustration of the stage ceremony of our ancestors is delightful for its almost infantine
simplicity. In Greene's *Pinner of Wakefield* two parties are quarrelling: 'Come, Sir,' says
one; 'will you come to the town's end, now?' 'Ay, Sir, come,' replies his adversary. And
in the next line, having, we may suppose, made as distant a movement as the narrow
stage admitted of, he continues, with amusing faith in the imaginative power of the
audience, 'Now, we are at the town's end, what shall we say now?'

We nowadays do not necessarily regard such methods as 'infantine', and
indeed the imaginative powers of modern audiences have been well schooled
in every kind of theatrical style and convention. Yet the writer just quoted
was evidently a discerning man, and it is at first hard for us to suppose that
he was far wrong about the simplicity of the Globe when one remembers
the matter of that thatched roof. The thatch, the tapestry, and the rush-
strewn stage: there come into the mind's eye the unmistakable features of a
cottage—can it be Anne Hathaway's? And below the thatch one imagines
the quaint criss-cross of Old English half-timbering—can it be Shakespeare's
birthplace in Henley Street, Stratford? One recalls the inn-yards where
the players used to act; the rumbustious scene paints itself for us in the
manner of a Christmas card, and persuades us to accept its implied simplicity of manner because it is so picturesque in effect. But is this, after all,
the right effect? Until quite recently it used to be believed that Shakespeare's plays were originally acted in the ordinary costume of his own day.
This we now know to be untrue—or at least a very misleading over-
simplification of the case—but it is still widely taught that the architectural background of the stage in Shakespeare's theatre was deliberately
intended to give the impression of the normal domestic architecture of the
day. Adams, in *The Globe Playhouse*, takes this for granted. 'The façade of the
tiring-house', he says, 'differed from its model, *a short row of London houses*,
mainly in having . . . curtains suspended in the middle.'[1] But there is no

[1] *The Globe Playhouse* (London, 1942), p. 135. The italics are mine.

reason at all for supposing that any feature of an Elizabethan playhouse was ever based on any such model. The idea is contrary to the very nature of Elizabethan drama. It is true that there was a small, though important group of Elizabethan plays which dealt with the contemporary scene; but the great majority of their drama was otherwise. Of Shakespeare's thirty-seven plays not one was set in the England of his own day: all were evocations of the romantic past or a romantic distance, or both; and all were intentionally so. Not even *Twelfth Night*, which one would take to be very contemporary and English in feeling, was allowed to come nearer home than Illyria. One may say that this was merely a nod in the direction of the prevailing Italianate fashion; but, even so, that fashion was itself the fashion of the splendid and romantic scene, and was the vein which inspired the greater part of all the work of every dramatist of the time except Ben Jonson; and even he, the great exemplar of English social satire, produced many works in a heroic or romantic mode. Temples, palaces, and towers were the characteristic backgrounds of the Elizabethan drama; the theatre was a place for 'Heroick and Majestique recreacions'.[1] Therefore, unless it can be shown that Elizabethan managers and actors were ignorant of any architecture but that of their own streets, or else had not the means or the imagination to provide themselves with any other, we ought surely to suppose that their theatres were furnished in a style at least suggestive of some sort of fantasy and splendour. In fact, we know that the imagination, the means, and the style were all at hand. And since a robust and fanciful ostentation has been typical of all popular entertainment from the most ancient times, one would surely expect to find evidence of it on the Elizabethan stage, of all stages.

The evidence is not lacking. 'Behold,' cries the preacher Thomas White, 'behold the sumptuous theatre houses, a continual monument of London's prodigality and folly.' He goes on to say that they are schools of vice, dens of thieves, and theatres of all lewdness, and if his testimony stood alone one might well brush aside his mention of sumptuousness as the exaggeration of a zealous Puritan who could not tell the difference between a piece of tinsel and an orgiastic carouse. But it does not stand alone.

---

[1] This phrase is found in the prospectus of an Amphitheatre which was under consideration in 1620; cf. Leslie Hotson, 'The Projected Amphitheatre' in *Shakespeare Survey 2*.

Here is another Puritan, John Stockwood, declaiming in 1578 against 'the gorgeous playing place erected in the fields'. 'Venus palaces!' cries Phillip Stubbes, echoing him. Sumptuous and gorgeous palaces already; and then a year or two later Stephen Gosson, in a pamphlet written against the theatres, still has to allow 'the beauty of the houses and the stages'; while Thomas Nashe in another, defending them, says, 'Our Scene is more stately furnished than ever it was in the time of Roscius. . . .'

The quotations given above range over a period from 1577, the year after the first theatre was built, until 1592. Since the theatres continued to prosper and were increasingly patronized by people of taste and culture, it is hardly likely that they decreased in splendour as time went on; and when in 1611 Thomas Coryat published, in his *Crudities*, an account of his travels in Europe, he had this to say of a theatre he visited in Venice: 'I was at one of their playhouses, where I saw a comedy acted. The house is very beggarly and base in comparison of our stately play-houses in England: neither can their actors compare with us for apparel, shews and music.'

Defenders and detractors alike, then, agree in this, that the theatres were decked out in some sort of splendour, and Nashe even believed the London theatres to have outrivalled the admired model of Imperial Rome. For in fact the Roman model, so far as there was a model at all, was the one. Johannes de Witt, the Flemish visitor to the Swan whose report originated the famous drawing, was particularly struck by what he considered a resemblance between that theatre and a Roman original, and the drawing is annotated with the corresponding classical references, expressly to point the fact. Ben Jonson, whose classically minded approach to the theatre was well known, has given us on the title-page of the 1616 edition of his Works, a picture of a classical *theatrum* as he supposed it to have appeared (Plate 48). The picture is clearly founded upon information from antiquarian sources, but the English engraver has restored it to what he and/or Ben Jonson must have supposed was its proper original form, by the addition of some huts over the top, after the style of those familiar huts over the theatres on Bankside.

Edmund Spenser, in his *Thalia*, speaks of 'the painted theatres'. Johannes de Witt speaks also of painting: he says that the Swan was 'supported by wooden columns, painted in such excellent imitation of marble that it might deceive even the most prying observer'. This is momentous information, but before following it up, let us look at another aspect of theatre painting. We have already noted in Chapter 2 that that roof called the Heavens, over the stage, is believe to have been ornamentally painted, probably with stars, suns, moons, or with allegorical and zodiacal figures. Adams quotes a fascinating list of references to the painted ceiling above the actors' heads, as for instance this, from Dekker's *The Whore of Babylon*:

> 3 KING.    Can yonder roof, that's nailed so fast with stars
> Cover a head so impious, and not crack?

and from Massinger's *Very Woman*:

> ALMIRA.    —But look yonder!
> Amongst a million of glorious lights
> That deck the heavenly canopy, I have
> Discerned his soul, transformed into a star.
> Do you not see it?
> LEONORA. Lady!
> ALMIRA.    Look with my eyes
> What splendour circles it! The heavenly archer
> Not far off distant, appears dim with envy,
> Viewing himself outshined.

A similar reference occurs in *The Silent Woman*, III. i. Captain Otter, the hen-pecked sportsman, is complaining of his wife's unreasonable attitude in the matter of bulls and bears. His friend Clerimont says:

> CLER.    Ay, she must hear argument. Did not Pasiphae, who was a queen, love a bull:
> And was not Calisto . . . turn'd into a bear, and made a star, mistress Ursula, in
> the heavens ?
> OTTER.    O lord! that I could have said as much!
> I will have these stories painted in the Bear-garden, *ex Ovidii metamorphosi*.

If this is not a reference to a painted Heavens in the Bear-garden it must refer to some other painted decorations there (presumably of classical subjects) which were topical at the time of the play's original production, either because they were just being done or else because they were in some special way a feature of that house; one might suppose them as being painted around the parapet of the middle gallery, very like those scenes that are painted in a primitive and boisterous style upon the fascia of roundabouts and booths at fairgrounds today. Indeed, one should bear this style always in mind when imagining the ornament of the Elizabethan stage. One should be on one's guard against supposing a refinement of taste beyond what a journeyman painter could do out of his copy-book. A good example of the vernacular style of painting in the period can be seen in Plate 61 and it falls very aptly upon the present subject, for it shows nothing less than a ceiling painted as a Heavens, still existing today in its original colours. Here we see, among cushiony white clouds, allegorical figures of the sort referred to in the plays, and behind them a blue firmament 'nail'd so fast with stars'. It is very likely indeed that just such a painting as this stood out over the stage at the Globe, and if so, this ceiling may be regarded as a unique original relic, at one remove, of the Elizabethan stage.

This ceiling is believed to be the work of itinerant Flemish painters,[1] which in itself would be typical of the time in England. Almost the whole taste of painting, engraving, and architecture in Elizabethan and Jacobean England was influenced by the Flemish style, even when it was not actually executed by Flemish artists. The names of Visscher, Hondius, and Gheeraerts meet us at every turn of portraiture or topography. Shakespeare's own portrait is by Martin Droeshout, a Fleming settled in London; and it is Johannes de Witt, the Flemish traveller, who tells us of the marble-painted pillars at the Swan. So we take up this detail again, which I referred to above as momentous information, and following it we find that it leads us again to Flanders, for the use of wooden columns painted like marble was very common in the decoration of Flemish theatres. A feature of Flemish town life at this time was its traditional theatre, which was organized by private societies called 'Chambers of Rhetoric' or *Rederyker* societies. It was their business to celebrate great public occasions by performances or recitals in verse and music, upon stages specially designed in a (usually) sumptuous baroque style. The appearance of these stages has been recorded in many engravings, and it was as long ago as 1889 that Wilhelm Creizenach suggested that there was an important connection between these stages and the theatre of Shakespeare's London. It is surprising that so little notice was taken of his opinion at the time, but of

[1] Cf. article by Oliver Hill in *Country Life*, 23 Jan. 1948.

recent years the trend of research has come with more and more emphasis
to confirm his view. Here, surely, is the 'Heroick and Majestique' style we
have been seeking, and it is not confined only to the engravings of theatres

A dais with balusters painted on flat boards. This not only indicates
the style of popular ornamentation likely at the theatres, but also
suggests the treatment of the gallery palings at the Swan (cf.
Plate 3)

From Turberville's *Noble Arte of Venerie* (1576)

and triumphal arches in the streets of Brussels and Antwerp, for some of
the most elaborate examples of it were erected not in Flanders at all, but
as triumphal arches in the streets of London to celebrate the coronation
procession of James I in 1604. These grandiose façades were embellished

with allegorical devices by Dekker, Middleton, and Jonson; Edward Alleyn appeared as the Genius of the City to speak the verses of welcome to the King; and Shakespeare himself, with the other members of his Company, the King's Men, received a bounty of scarlet cloth to make his livery for the occasion.

Some of these triumphal arches are shown in Plates 34 to 39 and they should be compared not only with the examples from Flanders (Plates 32, 33) but also with the ornamental title-pages to English books (Plates 47, 48). This was the accepted high style of the time, and it would indeed have been surprising if it had not found its way into the playhouses.[1]

The theatres were prosperous, scenic painters and builders were available with their Flemish copy-books at hand; the baroque style was paramount, the audience expected it, and actors everywhere else in Europe flourished in it. Moreover, our particular evidence confirms the detail of marbled and allegorical painting, and of sumptuousness in the Elizabethan theatre. In view of all this it should be difficult to prove, not that this was in fact the style with which the Elizabethan stage was embellished, but rather that any other style was ever likely to have been considered.

Upon stages of this sort, then, arrayed with pillars, pilasters, posts, and 'carved proportions', painted in marbling and in bright colours, picked out with gilding and hung with arras and curtains, the plays were mounted. We are well informed of the accessories that further enriched them. We know the details of Henslowe's property room at the Rose from his famous inventory of March 1598. I here reprint the selection given in modern spelling by Dr. G. B. Harrison:[2]

i rock, i cage, i tomb, i Hell mouth.
i tomb of Guido, i tomb of Dido, i bedstead.
viii lances, i pair of stairs for Phaeton.

---

[1] In Vol. II of his *Early English Stages* (London, 1963), Dr. Glynne Wickham contributes valuably to this argument with many examples including pictures of the processional cars used in the Lord Mayor's Show in London in 1616. Stow, in *The Survey of London* (1598), tells us that in his youth a large area in the Leadenhall was 'reserved for the most part to the making and resting of the pageants showed at Midsummer in the watch' (i.e. the procession of the St. John's Watch on Midsummer Eve). He says further that 'the lofts above were partly used by the painters in working for the decking of pageants and other devices, for beautifying of the watch and the watchmen . . .'. Stow was born in or around 1525, so this would presumably refer to the years until about 1550.

[2] In *Introducing Shakespeare* (1966 ed.), p. 141.

ii steeples, & i chime of bells, & i beacon.

i heifer for the play of Phaeton, the limbs dead.

i globe, & i golden sceptre; iii clubs.

ii marchpanes, & the City of Rome.

i golden fleece; ii rackets; i bay tree.

i wooden hatchet; i leather hatchet.

i wooden canopy; old Mahomet's head.

i lion skin; i bear's skin; & Phaeton's limbs & Phaeton's chariot; & Argus' head.

Neptune's fork and garland.

i 'crosers' staff; Kent's wooden leg.

Iris head, & rainbow; i little altar.

viii visards; Tamberlain's bridle; i wooden mattock.

Cupid's bow, & quiver; the cloth of the Sun & Moon.

i boar's head & Cerberus' iii heads.

i Caduceus; ii moss banks, & i snake.

ii fanes of feathers; Bellendon stable; i tree of golden apples; Tantalus' tree; ix iron
    targets.

i copper target, & xvii foils.

iiii wooden targets; i greeve armour.

i sign for Mother Redcap; i buckler.

Mercury's wings; Tasso's picture; i helmet with a dragon; i shield, with iii lions; i elm
    bowl.

i chain of dragons: i gilt spear.

ii coffins; i bull's head; and i 'vylter'.

iii timbrels; i dragon in Faustus.

i lion, ii lion heads; i great horse with his legs: i sackbut.

i wheel and frame in the Siege of London.

i pair of wrought gloves.

i Pope's mitre.

iii Imperial crowns: i plain crown.

i ghost's crown; i crown with a sun.

i frame for the heading in Black Joan.

i black dog.

i cauldron for the Jew.

One hesitates to rifle this rich store for items to comment upon, but certain of them may require it. It should be noted that the 'Hell mouth' and the 'dragon in Faustus', for example, come straight from the medieval stage; that the 'City of Rome' and the 'cloth of the Sun & Moon' give rise to the idea of a limited use of painted pictorial backgrounds in certain

To cut off ones head, and to laie it in a platter,
which the iugglers call the decollation of Iohn Baptist.

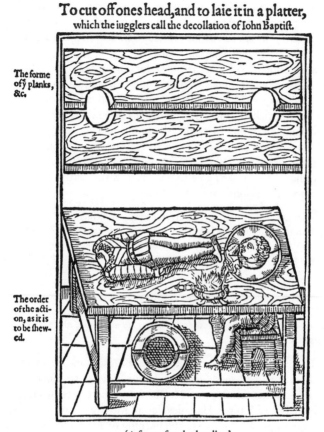

The forme
of ȳ planks,
&c.

The order
of the acti-
on, as it is
to be shew-
ed.

'A frame for the heading'
From Reginald Scot, *The Discoverie of Witchcraft* (1584)

circumstances (Heywood, in the *Iron Age*, made use of a Trojan horse[1]
which may also have been painted upon a cloth of this kind). The 'cauldron for the Jew' must have been the cauldron into which Barabas falls
at the end of *The Jew of Malta*; and the 'frame for the heading' was, as

[1] See Plate 62.

Dr. Harrison explains, a piece of stage machinery to produce the illusion of a beheading. It is interesting to compare this with the woodcut reproduced on page 73 which shows an old stage trick for appearing to knock off a man's head and serve it up on a platter.

In this connection the Elizabethan taste for gory realism should be mentioned. In their frequent scenes of battle, murder, and sudden death, the actors used to carry hidden bladders of pig's blood which spouted forth when they were pricked. They staged scenes of execution in which the entrails of animals bought from the slaughter-houses were plucked out from the 'victims' and exhibited to the spectators, as was done in earnest at the hanging, drawing, and quartering of victims by the executioner at Tyburn. Audiences were well able to reconcile all this with their 'Heroick and Majestique recreacions', and liked to see

a Hector all besmeared in blood, trampling upon the bulkes of Kinges; a Troilus returning from the field, in the sight of his father Priam, as if man and horse, even from the steed's rough fetlockes to the plume on the champion's helmet, had bene together plunged into a purple ocean; to see a Pompey ride in triumph, then a Caesar conquer that Pompey; labouring Hannibal alive, hewing his passage through the Alpes. To see as I have seene, Hercules, in his owne shape, hunting the boare, knocking down the bull, taming the hart, fighting with Hydra, murdering Geryon, slaughtering Diomed, wounding the Stymphalides, killing the Centaurs, pashing the lion, squeezing the dragon, dragging Cerberus in chaynes, and lastly, on his high pyramides waiting *Nil ultra*, Oh, these were sights to make an Alexander!

So wrote Thomas Heywood in *An Apology for Actors*, and he was writing not only of what he had seen (as he said) but of what he himself created upon the stage. In his tetralogy of *The Four Ages* there was enacted a long series of the deeds of Jupiter, Hercules, Jason, Meleager, and other heroes, from the beginnings of Olympus to the burning of Troy and 'the deaths of Agamemnon, Menelaus, Clitemnestra, Helena, Orestes, Egistus, Pillades King Diomed, Pyrhus, Cethus, Synon, Thersites &c.'. This cycle of more than Wagnerian proportions was very popular at the time when Shakespeare was writing *Cymbeline* and *The Tempest*, and continued to be put on at one theatre or another for many years. These four plays had little literary merit, and one may suppose their popularity lay principally in their abundance of spectacle. Their stage directions show, if nothing else, the stuff the Jacobean theatre was made of. Here, for example, are some taken at random:

Enter Busyris with his Guard and Priests to sacrifice; to them two strangers, Busyris takes them and kils them upon the Altar; enter Hercules disguis'd, Busyris sends his Guard to apprehend him, Hercules discouering himselfe beates the Guard, kils Busyris, and sacrificeth him upon the Altar, at which there fals a shower of raine, the Priests offer Hercules the Crowne of Aegypt which he refuseth. (*The Brazen Age*)

Two fiery Buls are discovered, the Fleece hanging over them, and the Dragon sleeping beneath them: Medea with strange fiery-workes, hangs above in the Aire in the strange habite of a Conjuresse. (*The Brazen Age*)

Sounde a dumbe shew. Enter the three fatall sisters, with a rocke, a threed, and a paire of sheeres; bringing in a Gloabe, in which they put three lots. Jupiter drawes heaven; at which Iris descends and presents him with his Eagle, Crowne and Scepter, and his thunder-bolt. Jupiter first ascends upon the Eagle, and after him Ganimed. (*The Golden Age*)

Sound. Pluto drawes hell: the Fates put upon him a burning Roabe, and present him with a Mace, and burning crowne. (*The Golden Age*)

Hercules sinkes himselfe. Flashes of fire; the Divels appeare at every corner of the stage with several fire-workes. The Judges of hell, and the three sisters run over the stage, Hercules after them: fire-workes all over the house. Enter Hercules. (*The Silver Age*)

Hercules kils the Sea-Monster, the Trojans on the walles, the Greekes below. (*The Silver Age*)

These four plays were unusual in the great amount of spectacle which they offered, but there seems to have been nothing unusual in the means used to present it. The chief mechanical aids were the flying throne which brought down the gods from the Heavens, or else the stage trap which let the devils out from Hell. Of the latter it is interesting to note how, for all the classical predilections of the age and the then available knowledge, which was not negligible, of the modes and manners of antiquity, the presumably classical Hades into which Hercules descended in *The Brazen Age* was inhabited by the same snout-faced, horn-and-claw devils, all fizzing with squibs, which Marlowe had used in *Doctor Faustus* and which were the popular stock-in-trade the theatres had inherited from the Middle Ages. Shakespeare called only twice upon this inheritance, in his first play and in his last. In *1 Henry VI* there are the Fiends which enter with thunder at the summons of La Pucelle; and in *The Tempest* there is Caliban, the 'freckled whelp hag-born—not honoured with a human shape', whose costume we know had fishy scales upon it. He was after all only a development of the old Vice, the comic devil of the Morality plays, in a Renaissance setting.

Shakespeare was not an innovator, as Ben Jonson was, and he was generally content to use material as he found it within the prevailing fashions of the theatre. But he did not have much use—and may, like Jonson, have had only scorn—for the Heaven and Hell devices of the popular stage. Both he and Jonson did, however, sometimes make use of the Hell trap in the conventional way for bringing in ghosts and apparitions, and there are two instances in Shakespeare of the use of the flying machine—though both of these are almost certainly interpolations by another hand, catering to the popular taste. The first is in *Macbeth*, III. v, where Hecate flies aloft seated in a 'foggy cloud'; and the second is in *Cymbeline*, V. iv, where Jupiter descends mounted on an eagle. It is interesting to note that Heywood's use of this effect in *The Brazen Age*, as given in the stage direction above, dates from within one year of the first production of *Cymbeline*, so that, if one production did not influence the other, both must have been availing themselves of a then fashionable invention.[1] Another point in this scene from *Cymbeline* is that in this case the Heavens ceiling through which the machine came down appears to have been painted, not like the sky after the usual fashion, but with marbling; for, as Jupiter ascends and disappears through it, one of the characters on the stage below says: 'The marble pavement closes, he is entered his radiant roof.'[2]

One has only to visualize for a moment what the spectacular dumb shows in Heywood's *Ages* plays must have looked like in reality, bearing in mind what a lot of them there were to be got through in each play, to realize that they must have been dealt with in a very summary fashion. It was all very much of a pasteboard parade; but it is from studying the constant

[1] There is a design by Inigo Jones showing Jupiter mounted on an eagle in the masque 'Tempe Restored', in 1632; cf. Allardyce Nicoll, *Stuart Masques* (London, 1937), fig. 45.

[2] This tallies with a further reference, in *Timon of Athens*, IV. iii, where Timon speaks of Heaven as 'the marbled mansion all above'. I suppose one must be on one's guard against reading too much into such metaphors, but I am inclined to wonder whether, since both *Cymbeline* and *Timon* are dated at about the time when the King's Men began to play at the 'private' Blackfriars theatre, the Heavens there might have been a marbled one.

factors of popular taste at this level, rather than the masterpieces of exceptional men like Shakespeare and Jonson, that we are likely to learn most about the basic character of this theatre. We find that it was violent, ornate, fantastic, abundant in poetic and processional emblems, and very noisy. Some of the effects which the Elizabethans set out to achieve were so far removed from our own tastes that they cannot be judged by our theatrical standards at all. For instance, we should miss altogether the significance of the emblematic imagery which it was an intellectual fad of that time to read and decipher. *Enter Rumour, painted full of tongues*, is an image which we understand at once when seen *in words* at the beginning of *2 Henry IV*, but it may be doubted whether we should at once 'read' the significance of the costume if it were newly shown to us, without a written explanation, on the stage. Fame with her trumpet, or sometimes for good measure with two (see Plates 31 and 50), we can easily understand, but Shame with a *black* trumpet, in the early play of *Cambyses*, has a distinction we might miss.

This emblematic method was particularly applicable to the design of costumes, and was developed to a high degree in masques and other courtly shows, so that the details of which a dress was composed might be studied, and its symbols well digested by the spectator. Thus the figure representing Sleep in 'The Vision of Twelve Goddesses', a Court masque given in 1604, was shown wearing 'a white thin Vesture cast over a black, to signify both the day and the night, with wings of the same colour, a Garland of Poppy on his head; and instead of his ivory and transparent horn, he was shewed bearing a black wand in his left hand and a white in the other'. What nowadays should we make of those white and black wands, with their distant classical reference to the Gates of Horn and Ivory which opened from the House of Dreams?

It is appropriate to bring in some mention of the Court masques at this point, because although they were in themselves an exceptional and luxurious form of private entertainment, not of the same family or derivation as the public stage, yet their forms and methods were reflected on the public stage, and their poetic references were common to both. The masque which Shakespeare introduced into *The Tempest* was conceived in the same terms as the masques at Whitehall, and indeed the only recorded performance

Costume for a Knight Masquer in Lord Hay's Masque, 1607

of the play during Shakespeare's lifetime took place at Whitehall before the King. We may therefore look at Inigo Jones's design for the costume of Iris in Jonson's masque 'Hymenaei' (Plate 66), given at the Banqueting

House, Whitehall, in 1606, and know that Shakespeare's Iris, in the masque in *The Tempest* six years later, would have worn a very similar dress. As for Ariel, we may suppose that as an airy spirit he would have been dressed in pale blue, or perhaps like the 'Ayrely Sprites' of Inigo Jones's *Temple of Love* designs, who had 'Garments and Caps all of feathers'. In the latter case it will be understood that the association of feathers is with birds and lightness, and thus with airiness by way of its emblems, and not by way of an airy or spiritual appearance. In the same way, a Spirit of Air in Somerset's Masque in 1613 was dressed in 'a sky-coloured skin-coat with a mantle painted with Fowle and on his head an Eagle'.

The reading of emblems or allegorical 'devices' was closely allied to the Elizabethan conception of heraldry as it was presented at the spectacular jousts and 'barriers' which were a feature of Court life. In these the knightly champions, each splendidly armed and caparisoned in his chosen lady's colours, were led into the lists by damsels, and accompanied by pages who explained the meaning of the device and mottoes on the shields. Thus Sir Henry Lee, a famous champion at these shows, when he was growing old, appeared in a caparison

> . . . charged with crowns
> Oershadowed with a withered running vine
> As who would say 'My spring of youth is past'.

The atmosphere of this chivalric jousting is intentionally represented by Shakespeare in *Henry V*, where the knights compare horses and armour and comment on the devices of their shields before the morning of Agincourt. It is also echoed closely in two other instances: in the procession of the Greek knights returning from battle in *Troilus and Cressida*, I. ii (for it must be remembered that tales of the heroes of ancient Greece were visualized by the Elizabethans as chivalric romances in the manner of Chaucer's *Palamon and Arcite*), and more closely still in *Pericles*, II. ii, where the knights pass over the stage on the way to the jousting, and, as each passes, his squire presents his shield to the Princess Thaisa, who explains the device on it to her father:

> SIMONIDES. What is the fourth?
> THAISA. A burning torch that's turned upside down
> The word, *Quod me alit, me extinguit.*

SIMONIDES.   Which shows that beauty hath his power and will
             Which can as well inflame as it can kill.

At the end of the procession comes Pericles himself, clad in rusty armour
and carrying his own shield, which shows:

             a withered branch, that's only green at top;
             The motto, *in hac spe vivo.*
SIMONIDES.   A pretty moral:
             From the dejected state wherein he is,
             He hopes by you his fortunes yet may flourish.

This mode of romantic chivalry, which was summed up for the Elizabethans
in Spenser's *The Faerie Queene*, and which, as has just been said, was accepted
as the model by which the Elizabethans visualized the heroic Greeks, does
not appear to have been similarly accepted by them for the heroic Romans.
The general appearance of Roman armour was well known to the Elizabethans, and to some extent they made use of their knowledge on the stage.
Plate 45 shows how the Roman style of costume was used side by side with
Elizabethan and purely imaginary ones in a performance of *Titus Andronicus*
in 1595. But better even than this as a reference to the stage appearance of
Roman tragedy, and clearly demonstrating the manner in which it was
mixed with both contemporary and chivalric styles, is the series of small
insets representing the story of Brutus and Tarquin, with the Rape of
Lucrece, as it was presented, probably in dumb-show, in the streets of
Amsterdam in 1609 (Plate 26). Notice also in this how the proud tyrant Tarquin bears as his emblems the peacock's feathers of pride and the hammer
of tyranny. That he wears a turban is also interesting, since in medieval
drama this was the usual way of representing the tyrant Herod. Other
pictures of historic and fantastic costumes as the Elizabethans knew them,
and in the style in which they were probably used in many cases upon the
stage, are shown in Plates 47 and 48. The Speed title-page is particularly
worth noting in that it shows an attempt at historical research. I doubt
whether a 'Britaine' would ever have appeared in this guise on the stage,
but the 'Romane' certainly would, and the fact that two figures in this
title-page and two others in the Jonson title-page facing it show a distinctive
style of loose, open gown, which seems to be associated with the idea of
heroic tragedy, indicates that a garment of this kind may also have been

commonly used on the stage. In the bottom panel of the Speed design the Norman, although the detail cannot be clearly seen in this reproduction, is wearing long, pointed shoes of an historic medieval type.

Enough has now been said to establish the claim that the Elizabethan theatre, so far from being plain and simple in its appointments, was accustomed to shows of elaborate spectacle against a background orna-mented, perhaps very elaborately, in the baroque manner. We may guess, if we will, that much of this was in a garish taste, and perhaps, after all, much of it was 'infantine', as the Victorian writer quoted early in this chapter said it was. It was a mixed bag, in which Hamlet was jostled on either hand by Ralph Roister Doister and Old Hieronimo. It played to the allegorical refinements of courtiers, and to groundlings who, as Hamlet complained, were 'capable of nothing but inexplicable dumb-shows and noise'. Of the dumb shows we have seen something, and since noise has once already been mentioned as a characteristic feature of the public stage, it would be as well to point out that noise seems to have been enjoyed by the Elizabethan groundling as a pleasure in its own right. The German traveller Paul Hentzner said of Englishmen that they were 'vastly fond of great noises that fill the ear, such as the firing of cannon, drums, and the ringing of bells, so that in London it is common for a number of them that have got a glass in their heads, to go up into some belfry, and ring the bells for hours together for the sake of exercise'. Without taking this report too solemnly it is true that the plays were full, not only of the noise of trumpets and drums, as indeed one might expect, but also of the noise of gunfire which they used on every possible occasion. Shakespeare is full of it. Cannons are shot off not only in battle scenes, but also to give effect to merriment and carouse, as at the feasting of King Claudius in *Hamlet*; and it was the firing of cannon at Cardinal Wolsey's festivities in *Henry VIII* that burned the Globe down in 1613.[1] The acme of all cannonading on the

---

[1] *Drum and Trumpet, Chambers discharged* is the stage direction in *Henry VIII*. The term 'chambers', which is common, shows us that the theatres did not use the whole cannon for such gunfire but only a part of it, the firing-chamber, a sort of iron pot with handles, which was made to lift out of the gun for charging. Thus it is probably wrong to show (as in the Adams/Irwin Smith model in *Shakespeare's Globe Playhouse*, and in a drawing of my own in *Shakespeare's Theatre*) an array of ordnance in the over-stage hut. The more likely and disenchanting fact was a row of little iron chamber-pots, like mortars, pegged to the ground round at the back of the playhouse. The piece of burning wadding which set fire to the Globe was probably carried back and upward on a draught.

Elizabethan stage was the sea battle, and when in *Antony and Cleopatra* there 'is heard the noise of a sea-fight', that noise was of gunfire from the cannons just outside the theatre. There was at one time a fashion for seafaring plays, largely no doubt because of the rich opportunities for cannonading which they offered. 'The battle at Sea in '88, with England's victory', was to have been one of the attractions of *England's Joy*. And, in *The Silent Woman*, the old curmudgeon Morose who could bear no noise, being distraught at the uproar which his new wife had brought upon him, named among the noisy penances he would be willing to endure to be rid of her: 'London Bridge, Paris-garden, Billinsgate, when the noises are at their height and loudest. Nay,' he concluded to crown it all, 'Nay, I would sit out a play, that were nothing but fights at sea, drum, trumpet and target.'

## 6. TOWARDS A RECONSTRUCTION

'THIS may be so, but on the other hand. . . .' I am aware that the picture so far given of the Globe has been so hedged about with caveats, qualifications, and alternative hypotheses, that the reader may well ask at this point whether in the end he can expect any picture of it which will honestly approximate to the truth. I use the word 'picture' here in two senses. The picture in the mind is one thing: the reader creates his own, and it will not matter very much if it should be a little blurred in places. But the picture printed on the page is quite another. Here there can be no blurring. Statements must be made for better or worse, true or false. For this reason scholars have been suspicious of reconstructive drawings or models, and rightly, since the only certainty about any one of them is that somewhere it is wrong. But the question is one of degree. It may not be *very* wrong, and we ought to be able to create an image of the Globe which will at least be near enough the truth for most useful purposes—that is, until, as may happen, further hard evidence comes to light.[1] I find that I have become satisfied with a certain image of an Elizabethan playhouse in my own mind, and this I have drawn and show here between pp. 90–91. Perhaps it would be best to call it a General Accommodation on the subject, and I will briefly, below, give the reasons around which I have constructed it. First, however, I feel it necessary to say something about recent trends of scholarship on the Globe, in the light of which this General Accommodation may be viewed.

In this matter I find that scholars are generally divided into two groups, those predominantly analytical, and those predominantly aesthetic in their approach. Typical of the former, I think, are Richard Hosley and Bernard Beckerman. They work by a careful, detailed, and uncoloured analysis of texts, on the principle that the old synthetic method of lumping together all the various and possibly incongruous information from many different sources has been misleading, and, as Reynolds exemplified in his study of the Red Bull,[2] that it is now more fruitful to isolate individual theatres, such as the Globe, and study the character of only such material as is known to belong to that one place. Since physical differences between the theatres must have existed, this is a useful discipline; but of course it is obliged to reject much of the help that may be obtained from a suppositious, but surely acceptable, general character of Elizabethan stage usage; and thus I think the results of the investigation may be occasionally misleading, as in the case of Dr. Beckerman's implicit rejection of flying machinery at the Globe, noted above in Chapter 2. However, for the most part the information gleaned by this sifting, analytical method is probably less misleading than that produced by the aesthetic method, though the latter has the greater inherent advantage of being more stimulating to the imagination, especially of lay readers. The

[1] As I write this, the newspaper on my table tells me that a great find of manuscript notes and sketches by Leonardo da Vinci, no less than seven hundred pages of them, has just been made. Since such a thing as this can happen it is not impossible, even yet, that the lost 'plott thereof drawen' of the Globe stage, or something equivalent, may one day be discovered.

[2] *The Staging of Elizabethan Plays at the Red Bull Theatre* (New York, 1940).

two foremost champions of the aesthetic school in recent years have been John Cranford Adams (and later his friend and co-worker Irwin Smith) and Leslie Hotson. These have provided not only pictures and models, but also, in effect, complete systems of supposedly Elizabethan dramaturgical stylization to go with them. The systems disagree widely with each other; other scholars have widely disgreed with both; and so do I myself. I am unjust, I think, to mention others' theories like this, merely to say that I disagree, and without explaining what they are. But this is no place for detailed criticism, and in any case these stimulating books[1] should be studied in full. My wish is only to make the point that the primarily aesthetic and creative approach which makes these works so enjoyable and thought-provoking, combining scholarship with imagination, may possibly mislead because scholarship touched by the warmth of imagination can very easily and imperceptibly pass from study to insight and from insight to something very much resembling an act of artistic creation in its own right. Recognizing more than a little inclination towards this in my own work, I have to bid the reader keep a close eye upon me, while briefly I explain and defend my General Accommodation drawing.

One begins with the admission of compromise. For instance, even although Dr. Nagler could be right (though I do not think so for reasons given earlier) in rejecting the two posts on the Globe stage (cf. p. 19, above) it would still be preferable in my view not to accept this objection, since this would lead to a reconstruction dissimilar in appearance from the Swan drawing. As stated above, I feel obliged to accept the Swan as the essential visual control for a reconstruction, just as the Fortune and Hope contracts (Appendixes F and G) are the essential dimensional control. Reconstructions need not copy them exactly, but they should be within an arm's length, even if the stretch may sometimes be a bit long. In fact, acceptance is not difficult, for, as has already been shown, all the principal evidences (the contracts, the Swan, the visitors' reports, and the exterior views) do independently corroborate each other to a surprising degree. As for the Swan drawing itself, its testimony has recently been examined yet again, this time by Richard Southern, and again found to be reliable. Dr. Southern's

---

[1] Adams, *The Globe Playhouse*; and Hotson, *Shakespeare's Wooden O.*

researches have always been remarkable for an unusually perceptive combination of both the analytical and aesthetic approaches to theatre history,
and his article, 'On Reconstructing an Elizabethan Playhouse',[1] in which
he re-examines the Swan drawing, among other evidences, not only
demonstrates the validity of the drawing, but in doing so provides a
valuable insight (in both senses) into the most likely interior arrangements
of these playhouses, which have hitherto been overlooked. The two most
outstanding of his insights—the arrangements of stairs leading from the
yard to the galleries, and the corridor around the back of the middle
gallery—should, I think, now take their place in all reconstructions, as
they do in my drawing between pp. 90–91, which we will now examine.

The vertical dimensions are taken from the Fortune contract, and give
an over-all height, from ground level in the yard to the eaves, of 35 feet,
allowing 1 foot of thickness for flooring and joists for each of the three
galleries (which the contract does not mention). In plan, if we allow a six-
teen-sided polygon with each side on the inside at ground level having a
span of 11 feet, this will give the yard a diameter of 54 feet (as against the
55 feet width at the Fortune). If we now suppose the façade of the tiring-
house to be lined up on a chord enclosing three bays of the polygon (see
sketch, Plate 69), this would mark off for us a stage width of about 32
feet; and in depth, to middle of the yard (as at the Fortune), the stage
would be 23 feet from the forward line of the façade. The areas of the stage
and yard are thus smaller than at the Fortune, owing to the contracting
effect of the circular form as against the Fortune's square. The visual
effect given, however, is consistent with our controlling picture of the
Swan.

The time has now come to return to the matter of the two stage posts
in relation to the over-stage buildings (the Heavens) which they support,
and to the character of the tiring-house façade, which to some extent
they qualify. The diagrams on p. 88 show three alternative positions for
the over-stage structure. The diagrams are all drawn to the same scale,
and all assume a stage height of 5 feet 6 inches from the ground. (N.B. I
think now that in the large drawing between pp. 90–91 I have been a little
timid regarding the height of the stage, which, to be consistent with my

[1] In *Shakespeare Survey 12*, Winter 1958.

opinion as given in Chapter 3 above, should look higher than this. The diagram's height of 5 feet 6 inches is a better conservative estimate.)

I am assuming a Heavens with a flat ceiling under the hut, as shown in my large drawing. In diagram (a) this ceiling is set on a level with the floor of the top gallery. This makes the posts 20 feet high, an impressive size which such a small diagram cannot well convey. It is a comfortable solution which the earliest reconstructors all adopted and which seems to be supported by the Swan drawing. However, as can be seen, it will obstruct a great deal of vision from the top gallery not so much from directly in front of the stage, but more and more as the spectators come further to the sides. Furthermore, the hut by this arrangement sits so far down into the well of the theatre that it would not be visible at all from outside, as all the exterior views tell us it was. I am therefore not satisfied with this.

In diagram (b) the Heavens ceiling is set on the level of the eaves, the solution adopted by Cranford Adams. The visibility problem for the top gallery is thus entirely solved; so also is the problem of the exterior view. The problem remaining is what happens above the level of the upper stage (which may for our present purposes be supposed to run at the level of the middle gallery of the auditorium). Adams here places a third gallery in the tiring-house façade which he identifies as the 'top' or high place called for in certain Elizabethan plays. (In Shakespeare's first and last plays, for example; in *Henry VI: Enter Pucell on the top, thrusting out a Torch burning*; and in *The Tempest: Solemne and strange Musicke: and Prosper on the top, invisible.*) But, as already stated in Chapter 2, I am unable to accept this solution on account of the very vast proportions of the stage columns which would be required. On the present calculation these would have to be 29 feet 6 inches high. Adams, with a lower stage, makes them even higher. True, to build such high pillars in timber would not have been impossible, but such a size in such a context seems to me so improbable that I would prefer to seek another solution.

Between these two heights, the one too high, the other inconveniently low, there is a median. Midway within the top gallery one may strike a ceiling height of 24 feet 6 inches from the stage. A pillar of this height would still be high indeed, but not unmanageably so. The ceiling would not obscure visibility; the hut would be visible from outside the theatre;

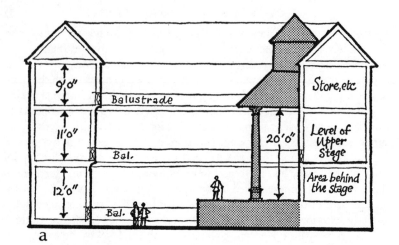

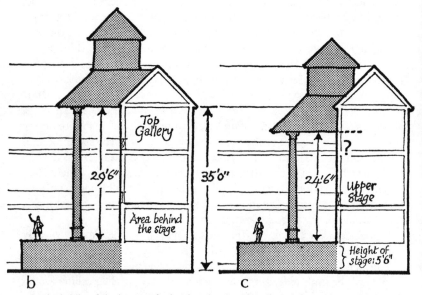

The height of the 'Heavens': sketches showing the effect of alternative positions

and the effect would still be comparable with the Swan drawing. This would satisfy me, but it leaves a certain query open at the point marked with a question-mark in diagram (*c*).

In (*a*) the two levels, stage and upper stage, are without complication. In diagram (*b*) the question of the top gallery can be resolved by supposing an upper stage, 'the top', as Adams has claimed. But in diagram (*c*) between the Heavens ceiling and the third gallery floor-level there is now left a narrow space, seemingly good for nothing, but which has to be dealt with in some way.

In the sequence of sketches in Plates 69 to 73, I have proposed a simple answer to this problem. The first (Plate 69) shows the upper-stage floor framed within the chord between the three-bay curve of the building. (It should be remembered that although in the diagrams, for clarity's sake, I have shown the floor-level of the upper stage lined up with the level of the surrounding galleries, this does not have to be exactly so. The tiring-house, in essence a separate unit 'erected and set up within the said frame' of the building, can take any convenient height of its own requiring.) The floor-level here is about 8 feet, which we have already found to be a useful height. Plates 70 and 73 show this floor arranged for use as an upper stage. But the Swan drawing demands a row of windows here. Accordingly (Plate 72), we erect a screen of windows along the front. But how high should this screen be built? What should happen at the level of the third gallery floor, where in the Swan drawing the Heavens roof interrupts the view, and where in our diagram (*c*) there is an awkward gap?

What has suggested itself to me is that *nothing* happens there. There need be no floor in the tiring-house at that level. Instead the upper floor can go higher, to the level of the ceiling, indicated in the diagram by a dotted line. The Heavens ceiling thus continues around, following the line of the round frame of the house, as can be seen in Plate 72; and the frontal screen stops above the window line, perhaps being finished along its top with some sort of decoration. What thus emerges is that the whole façade takes on the character of a typical Tudor hall screen, with its two doors below and its gallery above, as in the Middle Temple Hall, or at Hampton Court, or in many another great house hall with which Elizabethan players were familiar. And since it is clear that the musicians often used this gallery in the theatre as in the great houses, the music would be well heard from there over the top of the screen and under the sounding-board of the open ceiling. Such an arrangement, then, I have put in my large drawing. It may be that I have here made the screen too ornamental, with elaborately carved caryatids which would have been an expensive luxury. Perhaps this is where in my case the temptations of free artistic creation begin to creep in over the sober bones of study. But there has been a necessary case to make about such ornaments, as this book may witness; and we should not forget those 'carved proporcions called Satiers', which Henslowe had at the Fortune.

It will be noted that in the large drawing I have located the 'discovery space' or 'place behind the stage' in the familiar position, centrally between the two stage doors. This is usually justified by saying that although the Swan drawing does not show it, had there been an arras across it when de Witt visited the place he might not have suspected any opening was there. As an explanation it will do; but it leaves one nevertheless with an uneasy feeling that one is cheating the evidence. So I must confess that while I have adopted this solution for its general convenience, and because it has become so familiar by repetition that one may feel that if this was not the Elizabethan practice, then it *ought* to have been, my conscience is still a little uneasy. And what of that porch-like structure which has been supposed in Chapter 4 above? Have I, then, ultimately rejected this idea? I have not; but the truth is, I find a number of different ideas all simultaneously acceptable, and I think it is no bad plan to keep them all in play, as they may have been, for a longish time, on Elizabethan Bankside. On any one summer afternoon at the Rose or the Globe one might, surely, have seen one method employed at one playhouse and another at the next, a stone's throw away. That explanation, too, will do. Yet I will ease my conscience by providing one more drawing, from the same point of view as before, which the reader may overlay upon the other in his mind's eye and (since it is ultimately an aesthetic judgement) make his choice. It is seen on p. 91.

The tiring-house façade is here the same in principle, but plainer. On the upper level, within, it will be seen that I have divided it into three rooms. Thus there could be two Gentlemen's Rooms on the outside,

# The Globe Playhouse,
## 1599–1613

### A CONJECTURAL
### RECONSTRUCTION

**KEY**

AA  Main entrance
B   The Yard
CC  Entrances to lowest gallery
D   Entrances to staircase and upper galleries
E   Corridor serving the different sections of the middle gallery
F   Middle gallery ('Twopenny Rooms')
G   'Gentlemen's Rooms' or 'Lords' Rooms'
H   The stage
J   The hanging being put up round the stage
K   The 'Hell' under the stage
L   The stage trap, leading down to the Hell
MM  Stage doors
N   Curtained 'place behind the stage'
O   Gallery above the stage, used as required sometimes by musicians, sometimes by spectators, and often as part of the play
P   Back-stage area (the tiring-house)
Q   Tiring-house door
R   Dressing-rooms
S   Wardrobe and storage
T   The hut housing the machine for lowering enthroned gods, etc., to the stage
U   The 'Heavens'
W   Hoisting the playhouse flag

Position of Staircase

C.Walter Hodges
1965

with a principal room (for actors, or musicians, or perhaps a Lord's Room) between them. Below, centred between the stage doors, I have placed the curtained porch, which would be about 4 or 5 feet deep from the façade wall, where there may be either a third central door, as in the Fludd

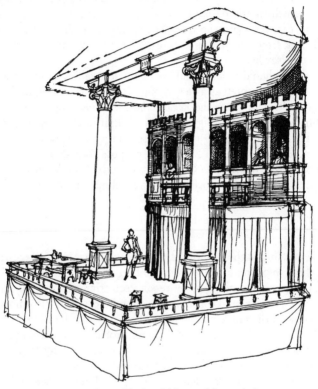

A tiring-house (the 'porch' hung with curtains)

picture (Plate 18), or a blank wall. But now on each side, borrowing Richard Hosley's idea of a continuous curtain or arras, I have joined the front of the porch back to the façade wall with a hanging running on a rail at a shallow angle on each side, hiding the stage doors within it. Thus the actors can pass back and forth behind the hangings between the doors and under the porch, or ascend on to the roof of the porch by a ladder at the back of it. (I have imagined here that only the porch top is roofed, not the two curtained extensions at the sides, which are open, and the gentlemen in the windows above can see down into them.) Around the porch top is a light railing—which might be anything else, a battlement, say, or a craggy mountain top. So again the imagination begins to flush, and it is time to pull back from further conjectures. I have shown other treatments of this façade elsewhere.[1]

Something should now be said about the low railing around the stage. This is usually accepted as a fact, though it remains a trifle puzzling. The chief authorities for it are the *Roxana* and *Messallina* stages, supplemented by John Webb's 1632 design for the Cockpit-in-Court stage, where a similar but very low railing is shown, seemingly a survival from an older tradition, since it seems to have little purpose. But there is also a clear reference to this railing in a Globe play of 1604, Middleton's *Black Book*, where Lucifer enters from below the stage, climbs up on to it and says:

> And now that I have vaulted up so high
> Above the stage rails of this earthen globe
> I must turn actor . . .

What is puzzling is the purpose of this railing. It has been suggested that it was there to prevent people from climbing on to the stage from the yard and interrupting the play, as, by report, sometimes happened. But even if this were a nuisance so constant as to require constant discouragement, which I doubt, the rail would be more likely to assist the climbers by providing a hand-hold than to hinder them. Probably its real purpose on a crowded stage would have been to help the actors visually to judge their distance from the edge of the stage. I accept it as that.

I show one trapdoor into Hell, centrally placed in the stage. I am aware that arguments have been advanced for several traps in various positions, but I am not convinced of the need for more than one.

I have indicated in the drawing the crowded character of the backstage area, full of old stage properties and costumes. It is very unlikely that such

---

[1] Cf. coloured drawings in *Shakespeare's Theatre* (London, 1964).

a restricted space would have been able to store all the gear collected in even two or three years of professional life, let alone two or three decades, and I assume that there must have been some sheds or other accommodation owned or rented nearby. Hollar's engraving of the Second Globe shows such a building close against the back of the theatre. With the quick-change repertory system of the Elizabethan stage, all gear would presumably have had to be stored near at hand. And so the imagination breaks loose again, wandering outside, round at the back, where all sorts of stuff lies spread out on the trodden ground, being got ready for tomorrow's new play. Propped against the wall by the tiring-house door two or three pieces of canvas battlement are awaiting a touch of paint. Under a nearby shed, by a carpenter's bench, two of the theatre servants are greasing a squeaky chariot wheel.

But this chapter was not meant for fancies of this kind.

## 7. THE GLOBE RESTORED

In all the foregoing I have tried to steer a middle course between two opinions of the Globe; the old one, that it was a quaint proto-theatre whose rustic limitations might best be allowed to stay where they look so well, in the pages of a picture-book; and a new one, that it was a theatre so excellently adapted to bring out all that is best in dramatic art that its loss was a calamity and its restoration is greatly to be desired. If I must choose between the two I will certainly choose the second, for reasons which will perhaps come better at the end of this chapter than here at the beginning; but I am none the less ready to suspect that if I could be carried back over those 350 years and set down among the crowd jostling into the Globe I might, on getting inside, and after my curiosity had

abated, find myself perhaps a little more disappointed than I would
happily admit, even to myself. Supposing it turned out, after all, that the
appointments of the stage and tiring-house were meagre, the painted
decoration wretchedly vulgar, even the famous marbling poorly done, by
the standards of later times? However, it would be quite a while before
my curiosity began to abate. To be taken back for one day to the Globe,
to see, to verify, to correct, and at last to know the truth about this old
building is a thing for which William Archer once said he would willingly
give a year of his life; and I would willingly accompany him upon the same
terms, carefully adding, however, as he did, that in bidding for the impossible one can afford to be generous.

That the possiblity of disappointment exists is because to have speculated
upon the probable facts of the Globe even for a little while is to have given
play to the historical imagination in a soil so rich, and so well cultivated
by great artists, that the reality even at its best would have difficulty in
living up to the fantasy that can grow upon it in one's mind. If, therefore,
one wishes to re-create the Globe, either by visiting it in imagination or
by building a replica of it, upon whatever scale, one ought to be sure what
it is that one is setting out to do. For modern playgoers one would hardly
wish to revive the conditions of the Elizabethan auditorium, even if
modern fire and safety regulations permitted it, any more than one would
wish to have in one's home the conditions of the Elizabethan kitchen,
however good the food. But following an increasingly important field of
taste there is a place in the modern theatre for the restoration of certain
features of the Elizabethan stage method, as I shall argue. And there is
also, I think, for purposes other than playgoing alone, a requirement for
the full-scale restoration of the Globe itself, as near as can be done, as a
historical (or quasi-historical) exhibit, as a national memorial to a uniquely
great episode in human sensibility, as a research tool, and, last but not
least, simply as a pleasure. For such it would surely be, and not only to a
few scholars, but to a large public for whom the whole matter continues
to hold a strong fascination. Let the wind of fancy blow upon it only for a
moment, and the life of it springs into flame, transforming the dry sticks
of historical fact into a bonfire of enthusiastic imagination. In such a way
I am tempted at this point to gather together all the themes of this study

and use them (since no actual reconstruction has yet been ventured upon) to rebuild the Elizabethan Globe in the fashion of my own fancy. Having attempted a drawing of it in the last chapter, I would now try to convince myself of its actuality.

I would begin by enticing the reader to come with me along a Bankside which looks very like the one we can follow in Hollar's engraving. I think I would like to make it very early in the morning, just in the gloom of dawn. We should only faintly see the clustered boats lying on their sides over there in the mud. The tide would be low. There would be two or three swans palely discernible, drifting downstream. There would be candlelight moving about in a house nearby, and a few lamps showing across the water within the big shadow of the town. At Paris Garden Stairs, a little way ahead of us, one can hear some man, early abroad, hailing a waterman to take him over to the city. His voice echoes. All being so shadowy at this hour, there is nothing, not even the strangeness of dress, which need be seen clearly enough to puzzle the perception. Not even as it gets lighter, and as, having turned away from the water a short distance down a lane, we arrive at the blank exterior of what seems to be a round building and which, being set as it is at the loose end of a few houses with some trees near by, reminds us a little of a gas-holder on the outskirts of a country town, not even this at present offers enough detail to dissipate belief. We do not notice what the building is made of, whether of wood or concrete. We notice a door, however. It stands ajar, and creaks a little backwards and forwards in the draught, whilst we are hesitating to go in. The creaking stops, we are relieved to find, as we push it farther open and pass through into a dark and empty yard. We are standing at last within the circle of the Globe. Looking upwards we see the sky grey within the encircling roof. In ten minutes from now, perhaps even less, it will begin to be light enough for us to see clearly at last what we have for so long been trying to imagine.

It is at this moment that I feel a touch on my shoulder, and turning to catch what my companionable reader has to say I find to my surprise that he is no longer with me. Instead there is a figure who, like one of Scrooge's midnight visitors, silently beckons me to follow him. It seems there is a place I must go to in one of the galleries, and as I turn I find—great heavens!—that the galleries are crowded! There they sit in silent rows all around the railings, rustling their note-books and pencils, cleaning and adjusting their spectacles, some wearing eighteenth-century periwigs, some in Victorian high collars, some in nylon shirts and other modern improvements, some from their graves and some from their beds and some from their seats of learning, all with their books in front of them, and all waiting patiently for it to grow a little lighter. I can just faintly make out one whom I take to be Edmund Malone; and there, I see, are J. O. Halliwell-Phillips and W. J. Lawrence, with Sir Edmund Chambers near by. And there are Ashley H. Thorndike, Harley Granville-Barker, and J. Dover Wilson; and here are Ronald Watkins and Maurice Percival from Harrow, and there again are John Cranford Adams and Leslie Hotson. There sits T. S. Graves with G. F. Reynolds, comparing notes with Nagler, Hosley, and Beckerman. Richard Southern I recognize, and Allardyce Nicoll; and I think those others must be Wilhelm Creizenach and Ludwig Tieck, sitting together. While eagerly awaiting the light—which this morning is taking longer than usual to come—we are listening to a little discourse in German from Karl Gaedertz, about how he came to discover the Swan drawing. Meanwhile I think I can just discern, in all the dimness over there across the yard, the shape of the stage buildings just as I have always believed them to have been. Almost certainly the daylight will justify me, when it comes. But now again there begins the suspicion that, like yesterday, it may not come here today—may not, alas, ever come here again . . .

Perhaps it will be thought that I have laid too much stress upon the uncertainty which obscures some portions of this subject. If so, it is only because it has seemed to me necessary to redress the balance wherein too much weight has been laid in the other scale, so that details which can be at best only conjectural have often been described as if they were certainties. It is necessary, I think, to hold the matter open as long as possible, so that new theories and fresh interpretations of the evidence can continue to enter in. For example, there have been two studies recently which both indicate a certain routine formality in Elizabethan stage practice, reminding one in some ways of the theatrical conventions of China and Japan. In one[1] Bertram Joseph has pointed out some strong links which he believes

---

[1] *Elizabethan Acting* (2nd ed., Oxford, 1964).

connected the art of the Elizabethan actor to the tutored and conventional delivery of the public orator; and in the other[1] Leslie Hotson gives reasons for supposing that the stage-keepers of the playhouses, who are usually imagined as holding a position more or less equivalent to the modern stage manager, were in fact masked attendants, wearing a sort of uniform, who

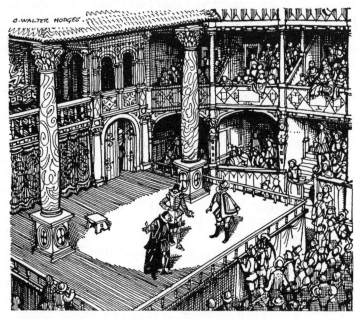

Conjectural sketch of a performance at the Globe. *The Merchant of Venice*, I. iii

were continually to be seen during a performance, arranging the proper-ties, drawing the curtains when needed (for these were generally drawn by hand, and not as in modern theatres by an invisible cord), and waiting at behest upon those privileged spectators who had seats upon the stage. If these things are true we must again make adjustments to our imagined picture of a performance at the Globe to give them room.

[1] 'False Faces on Shakespeare's Stage', *T.L.S.*, 16 May 1952.

But whatever details may still be undecided—and even if they have always to remain so—it must not be supposed that the Globe cannot be restored. If we combine all the things that are certain with all the things that can be accepted as more than probable, we can create, if not an exact, at least a characteristically true, portrait of the historical Globe. And although there are gaps in the evidence, we can, by studying the material which surrounds the gaps, begin to see evidences of character in the shape of the empty spaces themselves—just as an archaeologist, finding a small hole in the ground where some object, itself decayed to nothingness, has left its impression moulded in the surrounding earth, will fill this with plaster of paris, and presently recover a complete cast of the original form.

Plans to reconstruct the Globe are occasionally proposed, and it is reasonable to hope that in time one of them will come to fruition. A scheme to rebuild it at Stratford on Avon is at present[1] under consideration. Since this, if it is built, is planned to be used largely for research purposes, it is assumed that certain compromises often proposed, to house audiences under modern conditions, will not be necessary; for the truth is that there is no way of combining modern conditions with the conditions of the Globe without losing the essential quality of either one or the other, if not of both. It is often proposed, for example, that a modern reconstruction should provide seating in the yard. To do this it would at once be necessary to reduce the height of the stage, and so involve other dimensional modifications. No great matter, perhaps. One might also have to modify a little the access to the galleries, owing to the restricted flow of movement caused by the arrangement of seating. Again, no great matter. But, even so, the value of the theatre as a research instrument upon a basic point of stage-to-audience relationship will already have been reduced by the modification, since the yard will not now hold so many spectators, and the prices for admission to it will consequently be higher, if not the highest in the theatre, and this would mean a radical difference in the age, temperament, economy, and general character of that part of the audience. It is worth remembering that for a modern audience to stand, provided the admission is relatively cheap, is not an unthinkable proposition. For more than seventy years, at the Promenade Concert seasons in

[1] 1967.

London, people have regularly stood in queues all the afternoon, to buy their way in to stand at the concert all the evening. There is an active difference between this restless, attentive, packed-around audience and the more comfortable, critical, and composed audience of a theatre stalls.

Still perhaps a compromise in this regard, in a reconstructed Elizabethan popular theatre, may be thought no great matter, though some may have doubts. But there should be no doubts about the next compromise usually proposed. This is to put some sort of roof or domed skylight over the yard. To do so would involve such an alteration of basic character in the whole building as to make it doubtful upon what grounds it would be worth while continuing with the 'reconstruction'. For a beginning, it would bring with it considerations of heating, lighting, and ventilation hitherto irrelevant. But, further, it would in every sense change the atmosphere inside the theatre. The atmosphere of open air and open weather, good, indifferent, or bad as it might be, would give place to the wholly different air and acoustic of an interior. Birds would no longer fly down into the yard[1] in the evenings to pick up the crumbs left by the afternoon crowd. If this sounds merely a picturesque sentimentality, consider nevertheless what a very different setting it conveys in reality. Consider also that the roofed building, being thus no longer typically representative of its kind and of its place in theatrical history, would consequently lose very much of its intrinsic value and proper interest for modern visitors, since for them, be they audiences or tourists or schoolchildren or actors or antiquarians, the differentiating flavour would be gone. There would not be that particular quality of light and air descending from above into the

[1] DUNCAN.                          This castle hath a pleasant seat; the air
                  Nimbly and sweetly recommends itself
                  Unto our gentle senses.
   BANQUO. This guest of summer, the temple-haunting martlet, does approve
                  By his loved mansionry, that the Heavens breath
                  Smells wooingly here: no jutty, frieze,
                  Buttress nor coign of vantage, but this bird
                  Hath made his pendant bed and procreant cradle. . . .
                                                                        *Macbeth*, I. vi
It must be supposed that in thatched buildings having so many jutties and coigns of vantage as the old playhouses, there would have been many, perhaps too many, good places for nesting birds; and it is possible that, at the Globe, Banquo's audience could have seen the swallows nesting under the eaves as these well-known lines were spoken.

deep arena encircled by its three surmounting tiers of wooden cloisters; one would not sense the coolness of the lower galleries standing in shadow as the sunlight moved round above, till at evening the sunset would lie level on the thatched roof, the yard beneath gathering itself in darkness. There would only remain an indoor theatre dressed up in an old fashion and possessing, as a theatre, modern disadvantages not compensated by any ancient quality. Such a quality may perhaps best be illustrated from the world of music. Formerly (and not long ago) the harpsichord and the counter-tenor voice were, as instruments, generally thought to have no further claim upon life except as quaint antiquities, and the music of Monteverdi and his peers no audience, except for a few recondite musico-logists. But all that has changed. With only the blowing off of a little dust we have found that the complete world of baroque music lives as bright as ever, a perfected art, and the harpsichord is not, as was ignorantly thought, only a poor precursor of the piano, but has a pure quality of its own which the piano does not seek to imitate any more than the oboe imitates the clarinet, and which is indeed a more suitable instrument than the piano for performing the great repertory of its own earlier time. So it may be with a restored Globe, for the great repertory of Elizabethan plays and music.

The modern proscenium theatre has now reached the limit of its physical possibilities. Its wide range of visual effects (which is the characteristic it has chosen to develop above all others) has been supplemented by that of the cinema, and this again will sometime, perhaps even soon, be increased by the range of the three-dimensional colour-movie. All this, which has now become a special sort of theatre, conceived more and more in terms of dramatic pictures, has been brought to our very firesides by television, which again is likely to increase the range of its effects so widely that one may suppose the whole capacity of drama from the visual point of view is soon to be complete. And yet the more this side of the theatre develops, the more noticeable it becomes that one whole section of the theatrical scale is being left out, simply because it is incompatible with the production of this kind of effect. For instance, it is well known that the cinema, for all its wealth of technical accomplishment, is quite unable to do justice to the simple picture of an orchestra of any size playing anything at all, be it the *Tannhäuser* overture or 'Three Blind Mice'. A purely musical event is simply not cinema material. Neither is ballet. Not all the cunning of colour photography nor of changeable camera angles is able to disguise the fact that, to enjoy a ballet, it is necessary to be sitting personally in view of the actual dancers, to see all their movements related to the whole fixed space of the floor they are dancing upon, and above all to know that one is seeing a complete, unique, and *unedited* display of an ephemeral art. The fact of an aesthetic magnetism between a performer and his audience is too well known to need re-emphasizing here, but what may need to be pointed out is that with each step of development in the progress of the more visual side of drama, a little of this personal magnetism has had to be sacrificed. There is no likelihood, nor any reason to wish, that the technique of the visually specialized theatre (in the widest sense of the word) will be discontinued or even modified. But it seems now that the time is ripe to develop separately that other type of theatre which is not so much concerned with the scenic effect of a whole stage, as it is with the direct experience of that sort of artistic enchantment by which actors can create an imaginary world upon an empty space. For this the ideal stage is one in which the actors can come out into a close relation with their audience, standing, only a little separated, in the midst of them, as they did in Shakespeare's time. There is nothing thin or meagre or colourless about this form of art, unless art itself is colourless or meagre or thin. Only it should not be compared for its effect with the effects of the picture stage, any more than sculpture should be compared with painting. It is a different thing, and seeks to provide a different sort of experience. The full range of its capacities we can hardly tell as yet, because after the neglect of 300 years this form of theatre is only just beginning to be used again; and in order to take it up where it was left off, it is being used at present mainly for revivals of Shakespeare. But if, in restoring the type of the great Shakespearian stage, the impression is given that it is being done only out of a spirit of antiquarian research, or in order to provide some quaint occasional novelty, it will be great damage to a good cause. For on such a stage one might now hope to see the development of an intelligent dramatic form in which the work of individual artists can be enjoyed as a concert is enjoyed, in a clear and concentrated space. The wish for such a stage is not a fad of antiquarian taste, nor does it imply that the 'picture-frame' stage is obsolete and needs to be superseded by the 'platform' stage. Both of these stages are desirable; but only one, the proscenium stage, is at present generally available. It is only as a first step towards developing all the potential richness of the other that I suggest it is now high time we had the Globe restored.

# NOTES ON THE PLATES

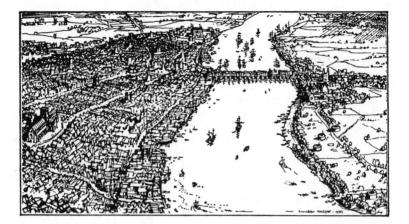

# NOTES ON THE PLATES

## Section 1. *The London Theatres*

1. LONDON FROM BANKSIDE, SHOWING THE GLOBE AND THE BEAR-GARDEN, *c.* 1616. From the engraving by J. C. Visscher.

Visscher's panorama of London, of which this is a part, was published in Amsterdam in 1616, but the precise date and nature of the information upon which it was founded is uncertain. It is not considered likely that the engraver worked from first-hand knowledge of London, but rather that he drew from previous maps and views, perhaps supplemented by sketches and verbal information from eyewitnesses. But from the evidence at his disposal, whatever it may have been, he was clearly satisfied that the Globe was a polygonal building. At the time of the first publication of the print this would have been the Second Globe, which was erected in 1614; but this does not exclude a possibility that the engraver might have worked from out-of-date information referring to the First Globe.

*Guildhall Library, London*

2. BANKSIDE, SHOWING THE PLAYHOUSES, 1600. From John Norden's
   revised version of his earlier (1593) map of London.

This rare representation of Bankside was described by I. A. Shapiro in an article in
*Shakespeare Survey 1* in 1948. Since then the accuracy which Mr. Shapiro claimed for it
has been confirmed by the discovery of other evidence which is published in the
Bankside volume (Volume XXII) of *The Survey of London*. The Norden map reproduced here is the only one which shows the playhouses correctly placed in relation
to one another, but it should be noted that the Rose is misnamed as the Star.

*Reproduced from the* Civitas Londini *map in the Royal Library, Stockholm*

3. THE SWAN THEATRE, *c.* 1596. Sketch by A. van Buchel, after a drawing
   by Johannes de Witt.

This famous drawing, often referred to as 'the de Witt sketch', is not in fact in the
hand of its originator, Johannes de Witt, but of his friend Arend van Buchel of Utrecht.
De Witt had visited London in or about 1596, and a letter from him describing the
Swan theatre was copied by van Buchel into a commonplace book, together with
this drawing. It may therefore be presumed that the drawing also was copied from
an original by de Witt, but of course we cannot be sure whether or by how much van
Buchel has altered it in the copying. However, it remains the only contemporary
picture of the interior of an Elizabethan playhouse, and its value as evidence is
corroborated by the many points (the Heavens, the flag, the pillars on the stage, the
three tiers of galleries, etc.) in which it tallies with other independent evidence.

The notes on the drawing were put in to point the comparison with the Roman
theatre which de Witt mentions in his letter. The appropriate part of the Latin text
is given in translation below:

There are in London four theatres [*amphitheatra*] of noteworthy beauty, which bear
diverse names according to their diverse signs. In them a different action [*varia scaena*] is
daily presented to the people. The two finest of these are situated to the southward beyond
the Thames, named, from the signs they display, the Rose and the Swan. Two others are
outside the city towards the north, and are approached *per Episcopalem portem*; in the vernacular, 'Biscopgate'. There is also a fifth, of dissimilar structure, devoted to beast-baiting,
wherein many bears, bulls, and dogs of stupendous size are kept in separate dens and cages,
which, being pitted against each other, afford men a most delightful [*jucundissimum*] spectacle. Of all the theatres, however, the largest and most distinguished is that whereof the sign
is a swan (commonly called the Swan theatre), since it has space for three thousand persons,
and is built of a concrete of flint stones (which greatly abound in Britain) and supported by
wooden columns, painted in such excellent imitation of marble that it might deceive even
the most prying [*nasutissimos*]. Since its form seems to approach that of a Roman structure,
I have depicted it above.

*University Library, Utrecht*

4. BANKSIDE, SHOWING THE THEATRES (with their names reversed) SHORTLY BEFORE 1644. From the engraving by Wenzel Hollar.

Hollar's complete panorama of London, of which this is the western portion, is the most convincing of all the views of the City before the Great Fire. Much, if not all, of it is based upon sketches made by Hollar from the tower of Southwark Cathedral (cf. Plate 5), and is therefore known to have the general authority of an eyewitness account. It does not follow, however, that it is to be trusted in all details, since the engraving was made not in London but in Antwerp where it was first published in 1647. Because of his Royalist sympathies, Hollar had been forced to leave London in 1644—incidentally the year in which the Second Globe was demolished. He took his sketches with him, but to supplement these and to refresh his memory of some of the details he seems to have used the well-known (and presumably approved) Visscher panorama (Plate 1). In particular, he has followed Visscher in naming the Bear-garden and the Globe from left to right in that order, thereby in fact confusing them. This confusion of names is fully dealt with in the article by I. A. Shapiro, and in Volume XXII of *The Survey of London* referred to in the Note to Plate 2 above.

Note on the far side of the river, between Blackfriars and Baynards Castle, a long roof which may be the roof of Blackfriars Hall, which had been made into a Private Theatre in Queen Elizabeth's time, and was occupied by the King's Men (Shakespeare's company) from 1608 onwards. Farther to the left Arundel House is marked by the waterside. Here Hollar himself lived and worked under the patronage of the Earl of Arundel.

*British Museum*

5. ORIGINAL DRAWING OF THE SECOND GLOBE AND THE BEAR-GARDEN BY WENZEL HOLLAR.

This, a detail from a larger drawing of Bankside, is here reproduced the same size as the original. It is in pencil, partly traced over in ink. It is to be presumed, though it is not certain, that the inking-over was also by Hollar's hand, though there is reason to suspect that this was done later than the pencil drawing. There are some small and interesting differences between this drawing and the plate (Plate 4) which was engraved from it. For instance, the drawing shows the Bear-garden (right) as appearing a little smaller than the Globe, which was probably due to the effect of perspective, since the Bear-garden was farther away from the spectator. In the engraving, however, this disparity has been 'corrected', an effect which is apt to happen unconsciously in details of this kind when copying from one drawing to another. It is also interesting to note, as I. A. Shapiro points out (*Shakespeare Survey 2*, p. 21), that the flagpole of the Bear-garden (right), which in the engraving is shown thrusting up as from the middle of the arena, appears in the drawing (where it is only faintly marked) to stand not inside but on the *outside* wall of the building, and just about where the far-side staircase-housing should be. In the same way, above the right-hand staircase of the Globe (left) there is a tall thing inked in, which, as Shapiro says, hardly seems likely for a chimney and may have been drawn originally as a flagpole.

It should be noted particularly that Hollar's representations of the playhouses are the only ones which show these buildings in what are known to be their correct proportions. All other exterior views of them show them as being much too tall and narrow. The question as to whether they were also round, as Hollar shows them, or whether for convenience of drawing he has simplified a polygon, can perhaps never now be decided. Lastly, and with reference to the confusion in the names of these two playhouses (see Note to Plate 4 above), it will be noted that the names were not indicated at all in this sketch and Hollar, working from it in Antwerp, had to rely upon his memory to tell him which was which.

*Collection of Iolo A. Williams, Esq.*


6. BANKSIDE, 1600. Detail from the *Civitas Londini* view.

This is a recently discovered view, and is to some extent based upon the Norden map shown in Plate 2. Both in fact were included in the same large view of London now in the Royal Library, Stockholm. A special interest of this representation is that the theatres are here seen as if half-buried among fully grown trees, as they may have been, and that the hut superstructures are shown sunk rather lower within the rounded buildings than they usually are.

*Royal Library, Stockholm*


7. THE CURTAIN THEATRE, SHOREDITCH, *c.* 1600.

This view of the Curtain playhouse in Shoreditch, part of a unique panorama of London from the north, engraved about 1600, was identified and published by Leslie Hotson in 1954. Its uniqueness apart, it has several important claims upon our attention. It is the only view besides the Hollar to show us the flanking staircase towers, and it is the only view to show the main entrance door. It also serves to corroborate the view that the playhouses were generally flat-sided polygons, not rounded. One further point may be of interest. The flagstaff appears here to be placed in a sort of battlemented tower, and not, as in the Visscher view of the Globe (Plate 1), at the apex of a pointed roof. One may thus be reminded of a passage in *Romeo and Juliet*, which is known to have had its first presentation at the Curtain. In the First Quarto version, in Act IV, scene i, Juliet cries out in despair to Friar Lawrence:

> Oh bid me leape (rather than marrie Paris)
> From off the battlements of yonder tower....

If it is right that in Elizabethan plays the word 'yonder' indicates a gesture towards something to be seen in the playhouse, then here 'yonder tower' is above the hut. It is therefore of interest that in all subsequent editions of the play the 'yonder' disappears, perhaps because what it indicated would have been inexplicable to readers not present in the theatre, or even because other theatres where the play was later presented did not have towers like this; and so the 'yonder' was altered, weakly, to 'any' tower.

*University Library, Utrecht*

## 8 and 9. DEBASED EIGHTEENTH-CENTURY VERSIONS OF THE GLOBE

Copied, probably at several removes, from originals already incorrect in themselves, such engravings as these served to puzzle the early Shakespearian investigators. The view on the left, dating probably from the first half of the eighteenth century, is believed to be an Italian copy deriving originally from an engraving by Merian first published in Frankfort in 1638. Merian himself probably took most of his material from Visscher (Plate 1). Visscher is, of course, the original of our other view (right), which was published in London in 1789.

## 10. THE LAST DAYS OF THE FORTUNE THEATRE. Engraving by T. H. Shepherd, 1811.

As with the Globe, so with the Fortune. Both built at the same time, one copied from the other; both burned down and rebuilt within a few years of each other; both in the end derelict, and their sites lost among tenements and breweries. The brewer's dray in this picture may count as a sort of rolling memorial; but it needs to roll a few yards further down the road, for it is doubtful if the building shown ever had anything to do with the playhouse. The real site must be just out of the picture to the right.

There is no scale on the map at the bottom, so we are obliged to make a rough deduction. Assuming the height of the doorways in the picture to be just over 6 feet (not counting the transom), we may judge the full width of the building at first floor level (Rose Alley on the left seems to pass underneath this) as about 36 or 38 feet. We know that the Fortune had an outside measurement of 80 feet square. Therefore the space marked on the map as 'Fortune Playhouse' could at best be only a part of the site. And why, after all, is there a street called Playhouse Yard some 50 yards down the road on the right? If we continue this Playhouse Yard *at its full width*, assuming the narrowing at the Golden Lane end to be due to encroachment, we shall find we have between Black Swan Court and Playhouse Yard, and Golden Lane and Thomas's Burying Ground, a rectangle of roughly 80 feet square, and this may have been the site of the theatre.

In very small print below the map, deleted because not legible in this reproduction, the following information is appended to the engraving:

The original Structure which stood here was appointed for the Nursery of the Children of King Henry VIII. The Lease was purchased by Edward Alleyn, Esq. Founder of Dulwich College, and he formed it into the Theatre, which he denominated 'The Fortune' and finished it in 1599. In 1621 the whole Building and the theatrical Property were destroyed by Fire. After being rebuilt it was offered for Sale in 1661, and then was of sufficient Space to afford twenty-three Tenements and Gardens, and a Street, now called Playhouse Yard, which at present exhibits a scene of Poverty, and is an Avenue from Golden Lane to White-cross Street.

## 11. THE FORTUNE THEATRE: A RECONSTRUCTION, *c.* 1836

This is the first methodical reconstruction drawing of an Elizabethan playhouse on record.

In 1817 the German writer and critic Ludwig Tieck visited England to gather material for a work on Shakespeare, and it is likely that while there he came in contact with those, such as the younger James Boswell, who were continuing the work of Edmund Malone; and so it was probably at this time that he took note of the Henslowe papers, especially the contract for the Fortune building. Some years later he was settled in Dresden where, with his daughter Dorothea, he collaborated with A. W. Schlegel in the latter's great translation of Shakespeare into German, which was completed in 1833. During this work Tieck had been giving much thought to the formal requirements of a stage for the production of Shakespeare's plays in the manner originally intended, a manner of which nothing was known except by inference and deduction. Tieck incorporated his ideas in a story, *Der junge Tischler-meister*, which he published in 1836. While working on this he was also in touch with the architect Gottfried Semper who had come to Dresden to build the opera house there, and he inspired Semper to make reconstruction drawings of the Fortune Theatre under his guidance. These, too, were published in 1836.

The reconstruction shown here is therefore a mixture of several influences: Tieck's scholarship, his view of an ideal Shakespearian stage, Semper's personal preoccupation with the German neo-Renaissance architectural style (of which he was the initiator), and all the rather solemn gaiety of German nineteenth-century Romanticism.

Tieck has provided a pavilion-like discovery space surmounted by an upper-stage balcony. The use of elaborate stairways which he here exploits is not truly Elizabethan, and indeed would have inhibited the free movement of large scenic properties, such as wall, beds, etc., which the texts sometimes call for; but it seems, incidentally, that Tieck was here the first to envisage the dramatic possibilities of the stepped form of permanent setting which in more recent times has featured importantly in the work of Appia and Craig, and of designers and producers everywhere

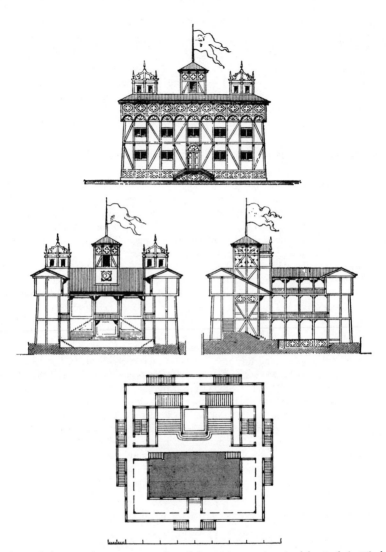

Plan and elevation for a reconstruction of the Fortune as imagined by Ludwig Tieck.
Drawing by Gottfried Semper, *c.* 1836

in the 1920s and 1930s, if not still today. It will be noted that Semper and Tieck have abandoned, if they ever considered, the thrust-out three-sided shape of the Elizabethan stage, although this is clearly to be deduced from the Fortune contract. From Semper's point of view there could have been no sort of sense in that. So he has rationalized the contract and designed a charming 'Old English Summer Theatre', as he and Tieck would have liked it to have been.

*Photo: Franz Rapp Collection, Dresden*

## 12. 'AN OLD ENGLISH INDOOR THEATRE', as visualized in 1836

Working with Tieck and his daughter Dorothea in Dresden was the diplomat and man of letters, Graf Wolf von Baudissin. He, too, was an enthusiast of the Old English drama. In 1836 he published his book *Ben Jonson und seine Schule* in which the Tieck/Semper reconstruction of the Fortune (Plate 11) first appeared. In the same book was included this imaginative reconstruction of an indoor or closed (*geschlossenes*) theatre, in the composition of which we must suppose Tieck to have had a hand. Allowing for the early nineteenth-century mannerism of the artist, it has to be conceded that on this evidence ideas have not moved very far in more than a century (though it must be admitted this is rather contradicted by the Pycroft drawing which follows here). Tieck's personal preoccupation with visible steps may be observed between the curtains flanking the central discovery space. Perhaps the most surprising feature is the use of the uppermost central gallery for musicians, a position re-affirmed by Adams (*The Globe Playhouse*) in 1943, and yet again by Irwin Smith (*Shakespeare's Blackfriars Playhouse*) in 1964. A comparison with Smith's Blackfriars reconstruction, independently arrived at, shows a remarkable similarity.

In his old age Tieck was given a pension by King Frederick William IV of Prussia, and went to live in Berlin. There in 1843 at the age of seventy he produced at the royal theatre in the palace of Potsdam a performance of *A Midsummer Night's Dream* in the Elizabethan manner: that is, it was produced uncut, without scenery, and on an open stage, but was embellished with Tieck's familiar flights of stairs. The music for this production was specially commissioned by the king from Felix Mendelssohn; and so in the end it is this familiar and well-loved music which remains in our ears to remind us of Ludwig Tieck's historical adventure with the Elizabethan stage.

*Clara Ziegler Theatermuseum, Munich*

## 13. THE GLOBE: A RECONSTRUCTION OF *c.* 1860

This mid-Victorian water-colour by George Pycroft was in its time a reasonable attempt to make sense out of the material then available. The Swan drawing and the Fortune and Hope contracts, with their express statements of three tiers of galleries, could not have been known to the artist, though he seems to have had some knowledge of Renaissance theatrical engravings, for he shows a high stage in the typical manner of the early street theatres. His idea of the Heavens seems to be based upon Malone's incorrect notion that 'pieces of drapery tinged with blue' might have been 'suspended across the stage to represent the heavens'. It was a shot in the dark, guided by a knowledge of the ordinary proscenium stage's use of sky borders. Accordingly, Pycroft's drawing shows a piece of drapery suspended on curtain rings across the stage. In front of this hangs a notice indicating the scene, a 'Plain near Shrewsbury'. This, a common fallacy in Pycroft's time, and one which is still sometimes credited, derives from a misunderstanding of the Elizabethan use of title boards. The nineteenth-century scholars supposed, seeing that no scenic illusion could be offered on the Elizabethan stage, that it must have been necessary to supply the want in some visual way; it seems not to have occurred to them that Shakespeare's plays, if played as written (which the Victorians did not do), automatically explain their own supposed localities as they go along. The extent of the Elizabethan use of title boards may be disputable, especially so far as the public theatres were concerned, but it is clear enough that they were not used to show individual scenes, but were supposed to indicate localities to be accepted more or less permanently throughout the play. Thus several doors would be marked each with the name of the person or place with which it was to be specially associated (cf. Plate 19). This was, of course, a variation of the medieval use of 'mansions', but although Elizabethan critics tended to frown upon its absurdities ('What Child is there', wrote Sir Philip Sidney, 'that coming to a Play, and seeing *Thebes* written in great letters upon an old door, doth believe that it is Thebes?') Elizabethan actors seem to have found it too useful to dispense with altogether. It seems also to have been customary at times (though again the extent of the practice is very questionable, and it may have referred principally to private performances) to hang up a board inscribed with the title of the play. It will be noted that Pycroft shows labels over all the entrances in the proper manner.

Pycroft's sign on the theatre wall seems, like his Heavens, to be based on Malone, who reported from William Oldys (1696–1761) that the Globe displayed for a sign 'a figure of Hercules supporting the Globe, under which was written *Totus mundus agit histrionem*'. Such a sign would, however, have been hung outside rather than within the theatre.

For all its shortcomings, the picture has many merits, perhaps not the least being that it demonstrates the discomfiture that waits upon even the best-intended of historical reconstructions in the end.

*Radio Times Hulton Picture Library*

## 14. THE GLOBE: A RECONSTRUCTION OF 1910

I have chosen this reconstruction by A. Forestier which appeared in the *Illustrated London News* in 1910, because it sums up very well the attitude of the most informed opinion at that time about the conditions of the Elizabethan playhouses, and indeed in many respects it is the opinion still popularly held today. Forestier was an artist who specialized in historical reconstructions, and it is difficult not to feel convinced by such an excellent example of his work as this. None the less, although the hurly-burly atmosphere of the auditorium is very well expressed (and it is typical of the date of this reconstruction that it should approach the subject so much from this point of view), the details of the stage background itself are imaginary, and are drawn not from original sources but from the deductions of nineteenth-century scholars and editors. In its general appearance the drawing is, of course, founded upon the de Witt sketch (Plate 3), but the addition of a curtained 'inner stage' and the angled setting of the side doors and windows are ideas which de Witt does not support. The attempt in such reconstructions to provide a sort of enclosed space at the rear of the stage derives, I suspect, more from a wish in the nineteenth-century mind to equate the Elizabethan stage with some at least of the habitual practices of the familiar nineteenth-century proscenium stage than from any evidence the Elizabethan stage itself has to offer. Other things which may be assumed to be incorrect in this drawing are the upper building over the stage (which was almost certainly built forward, overhanging the stage, so that the heavenly throne could descend on to the stage, in front of the background façade), and the rather plain appearance of the whole stage presentation—a typical Elizabethan play and playhouse is likely to have been decked out in a more florid and showy fashion than this.

*Illustrated London News*

## 15. AN OPENING FROM HENSLOWE'S DIARY FOR 1597–8

If Philip Henslowe's name is remembered as second to the Burbages in the theatrical fame of his time, it is perhaps only because he did not have the good fortune to be much associated with Shakespeare. He was the most enterprising manager of theatrical affairs of his day. He owned at one time or another the Rose, the Fortune, and the Hope theatres, and one other at Newington Butts. His son-in-law was Edward Alleyn, the great rival in fame of Richard Burbage. A famous collection of private papers belonging to Henslowe and Alleyn have been handed down in the muniment of Dulwich College, the College of God's Gift which Alleyn founded in 1617. The most famous of these documents is Henslowe's so-called 'diary', really an account and memorandum book. The opening from it shown in this plate is reprinted in clear with explanatory notes at Appendix C.

*Reproduced by permission of the Governors of Dulwich College*

## 16. PORTION OF A LETTER FROM EDWARD ALLEYN TO HIS WIFE

If the question is asked why, in books like this, so much effort is now spent in trying to reconstruct an ancient theatre, it may be answered simply by producing this letter. There are few historical documents which so immediately restore their writers to a momentary reliving, than the common, affectionate notes written between husband and wife. This touring actor writing home makes himself so real to us that it is an irresistable tantalization not to know what his London theatre was like. One must scratch and scratch, to try to find out. The letter was written during the great plague of 1593 when, the London theatres being closed, the players were touring the provinces. It was written from Bristol on 1 August. The whole text is as follows (the portion shown in the plate being indicated in the margin):

Emmanuel,

My good sweet Mouse,

I commend me heartily to you and to my father, my mother, and my sister Bess, hoping in God though the sickness be round about you yet, by His Mercy, it may excape your house, which, by the grace of God, it shall. Therefore use this course; keep your house fair and clean, which I know you will, and every evening throw water before your door, and in your backside, and have in your windows good store of rue and herb of grace, and with all the grace of God, which must be obtained by prayers; and so doing, no doubt but the Lord will mercifully defend you.

Now, good mouse, I have no news to send you but this, that we have all our health, for which the Lord be praised. I received your letter at Bristow, by Richard Cowley, for the which I thank you.

I have sent you by this bearer, Thomas Pope's kinsman, my white waistcoat, because it is a trouble to me to carry it. Receive it with this letter, and lay it up for me till I come.

If you send any more letters, send to me by the carriers of Shrewsbury or to West Chester or to York, to be kept till my Lord Strange's players come.

And thus, sweetheart, with my hearty commendations to all our friends, I cease from Bristow this Wednesday after Saint James his day, being ready to begin the play of *Harry of Cornwall*.

Mouse, do my hearty commends to Mr. Grigs' wife and all his household, and to my sister Phillips.

Your Loving husband,

E. Alleyn.

Mouse, you send me no news of any things you should send of your domestical matters; such things as happen at home, as how your distilled water proves, or this, or that, or any thing what you will.

And Jug, I pray you let my orange tawny stockings of woollen be dyed a very good black against I come home to wear in the winter.

You sent me not word of my garden, but next time you will. But remember this, in any case, that all that bed which was parsley in the month of September, you sow it with spinach, for then is the time. I would do it myself but we shall not come home till Allholland tide. And so, sweet mouse, farewell, and brook our long journey with patience.

## 17. THE 'PLATT' OF THE SECOND PART OF *THE SEUEN DEADLIE SINNS*

The 'Platt' or Plot of a play was a synopsis of the action. It appears to have been customary to have had the 'Platt' mounted on a board and hung up within the tiring-house for quick reference by the backstage staff during the course of a play; for it should be remembered that plays were only given for two or three days at a time, or even for single performances only, and not for runs as nowadays; so that it would be necessary for the back-stage organization to have some quick reference at hand for the prompt marshalling of costumes, properties, etc. The present example (which is reprinted for easier reference at Appendix D) was found pasted into the covers of a book, to serve as an endpaper, and the dark mark across the middle is the spine of the bookcover. The rectangular mark in the middle of the upper half is a hole in the paper, believed to be the hole where the platt-board was originally hung upon a peg in the tiring-house.

The play itself is a Morality, indicating by seven legendary examples the effects of the Deadly Sins. The First Part, which is lost, evidently dealt with the first four of the sins. In the Second, as is shown in the first item of the 'Platt', all seven sins take the stage together, but the last three drive in the other four (who have already had their turn) and then proceed to present their own examples. Two saintly characters, the monk Lidgate and King Henry VI, comment upon the action from time to time.

A feature of particular interest is that the actors of the play are referred to sometimes in the characters they personate and sometimes by their own names, e.g. 'Enter King Gorboduk . . . R. Burbadge, Mr. Brian, Th. Goodale. The Queen with Ferrex & Porrex and some attendants. . . .' From the knowledge thus gained it appears that this 'Platt' refers to a production given by a company which was occupying Henslowe's Rose around 1591–2. This must therefore have been a revival, for the author, Richard Tarlton the great comedian, had died in 1588.

*Reproduced by permission of the Governors of Dulwich College*

## 18. A MNEMONIC 'GLOBE THEATRE', 1619

This picture is an enigma. It is one of many diagrams in a long book of metaphysics printed in Germany in 1619, written by an Englishman in Latin and dedicated to King James I. It purports to represent a theatre, and bears the inscription that it is a 'Theatrum Orbi(s)', Theatre of the World, or Globe Theatre. It was first brought to the notice of Shakespeare students by the late Richard Bernheimer in 1958.[1] Bernheimer claims, with textual examples from Elizabethan plays, that it must be in some way related to some sort of real theatre, and shrewdly points out resemblances between the form of this building and the old-style covered tennis courts which were

[1] *Shakespeare Quarterly*, Vol. IX, No. 1.

frequently used as theatres. Following Bernheimer, Miss Frances Yates in a recent article[1] has gone further, and announces that this is in fact a representation, only a little altered, of the Second Globe.

The original author was a curious scholastic named Robert Fludd, and his magico-scientific book concerns the relation of mankind to the macrocosm and the micro-cosm. The section in which this engraving occurs is devoted to the discipline of memory, by means of setting up simple and familiar architectural arrangements (such as, of a theatre) whose features can be methodically identified with sequential pointsi n an argument, and thus used as a mnemonic aid in philosophic debate. That the book was printed in the Rhineland is not unusual, since this was the centre of the printing trade in north-west Europe at that time, especially when much pictorial engraving was required.

According to Miss Yates, Fludd insists that only real buildings, not imaginary ones are to be used in the 'art of memory'. He further specifies that when he speaks of a theatre he means 'a public theatre in which comedies and tragedies are acted'. If this were to be taken literally it would mean that this picture shows an actual playhouse in a familiar form. Yet it is not a typical public theatre because it is not round; and, besides this, across the front of the stage Fludd has placed five base-marks, where five pillars are supposed to stand, in positions which surely could not be accepted in front of any sort of stage; and indeed Fludd says of these that they are put there only for the mnemonic purposes of the book. Thus there are features in the engraving which do not belong to a real theatre, and Miss Yates takes advantage of this to go on and make certain modifications of her own, such as to alter it from a rectangular to a round building, etc., bringing the whole thing into line with the known shape and layout of an English public playhouse. She is not without some justification. It has to be remembered that whatever instructions were transmitted by Fludd to his en-gravers in Germany would have been subject to some uncertain amount of inter-pretation and alteration by distant foreign hands—one can see, for instance, a touch of typically German architectural detail about the roof and corbel of the curious bay window in the centre.

However, although by the time one has finished rationalizing it with necessary conjectures, one has weakened it deplorably as evidence, there still remain certain items in this picture too significant to be disregarded. Here is the upper level, here are the battlements so familiar in Elizabethan war plays, here the flanking entrances, the boxes along the sides of the stage (although the house is rectangular and the blank walls above the boxes are surprising and improbable); and in particular it is interesting and convincing to see a central doorway, a feature often postulated but never before shown like this in a supposedly English theatre of the time. Moreover, the peculiar central bay window is itself far from unacceptable as a stage feature, and

[1] *The New York Review of Books*, 26 May 1966.

may be compared with the projecting bay of the Brussels stage in Plate 25. One might vary the Fludd example a little, and suppose the bay window supported on pillars like the Brussels stage, and then closed around below with curtains, hiding the central door, thus forming a discovery space. Then indeed we would have a workable Elizabethan stage.

Altogether it seems that the picture, whatever it can be taken to mean, cannot be denied its place among the evidence; but what it does mean, how it should be interpreted, and how literally how much of it is to be taken, is at present very far from clear to this writer.

*Folger Shakespeare Library, Washington*

## Section II. Street Theatres

### 19. THE STAGE FOR *LAURENTIUS*, COLOGNE, 1581

This unique drawing shows an open-air stage erected for a play dealing with the martyrdom of St. Lawrence. The scenic arrangements are carefully annotated, and it would seem that this sketch is either an original design for the stage layout, or else (perhaps more likely) a record of a successful arrangement noted for use on future occasions. The method of presentation is recognizably medieval: but it is also similar to much Elizabethan practice in England, especially during the earlier period. But the method, as I have noted elsewhere in the text, was probably maintained in part even into Jacobean times; and indeed the atmosphere of this martyrdom play seems very similar to that of Massinger's *The Virgin Martyr* (which may be conjectured as having been acted around 1614, that is to say a date midway between 1606, when Massinger left college, and 1622, when the play was first printed). It may be noted that when this *Laurentius* stage was erected in Cologne, the early public theatres of Burbage and Henslowe had already been in existence for five years.

The *Laurentius* stage is shown as having been built around two standing trees, which may remind us of the two pillars in the de Witt drawing. The stage is supported on barrels, and its planks appear to be strewn with something, perhaps sand or earth, making pathway areas upon it; perhaps this was to deaden the noise of feet on the stage. Around the stage the old medieval 'houses' are represented by their doors (cf. the Note to Plate 13). The 'houses', from left to right, are allotted to the High Priest of Jupiter, Augustus, and Valerianus; then comes the Praetorium, and two thrones for Augustus and the Praetor; then the plinth of a statue, of which more is to be said below; next, the house of Hippolitus; then a prison; then the houses of Sixtus and Faustina; then an odd corner which seems to have been ramped up to represent a hill, the Caelian Mount; and on the right the gate supposed to be that of the Etruscan town of Capena. In the forefront left and right are the idolatrous monuments to which St. Lawrence refused tribute; on the left, upon the altar of Jove, the oil and wine which he would not pour stand ready by the sacred flame. The object towards the right centre is the gridiron upon which the saint was roasted.

Returning to the central plinth, this is marked as *Locus statuae SS martyris Laurentii*: 'the place for the statue of the most holy martyr Lawrence'. The curious thing is that this plinth is not built out on to the stage as other things are, but is painted on the scenic wall. It gives me to suppose that the actual standing-place for the statue was in the rear, behind the scenic wall, and that the part above the plinth was covered throughout the play with a curtain painted like the rest of the wall. At the end of the play, however, one must suppose that a statue of the martyred saint was exposed here, as in a niche, the curtain being then drawn aside; and it would be reasonable to think that the actor who had personated the saint would have taken his place here as the statue, behind the curtain. To complete the conjecture, it was probably a miraculous statue that moved and spoke.

*Photo: Oskar Fischel Collection*

## 20. PLAYERS IN AN AUDIENCE, Northern Italy, *c.* 1690. Painting attributed to Luca Carlevaris

The manners and methods of the strolling players can have altered very little in the hundred years from the days of James Burbage to the time when this picture was painted. An engraving made two generations earlier in Flanders (reproduced in Southern, *The Seven Ages of the Theatre*, Plate 6) shows a remarkably similar theatrical situation: the same high rope slung from the roof, for acrobats; the same tight-rope walker, with a performer sitting on the cross-trees; a performance in progress on the stage and an audience at the side. In the present instance, even the actors' costumes have retained the ruff and trunk-hose of the players of the earlier century.

Late as it is for an example (and the greater availability of well-painted pictures from the later period makes their inclusion tempting), this scene is relevant in other respects also, showing as it does an audience-to-player relationship very similar to that of the Elizabethan period. It is interesting to compare the side boxes with those of the 'Theatrum Orbi' in Plate 18. The two entrances in the façade at the back, though here scenically painted, are strongly reminiscent of the Elizabethan arrangement, and the comedy in progress, if the Harlequin is left aside, might very easily have come from Ben Jonson.

*By permission of the Wadsworth Athenaeum, Hartford, Conn.*

## 21. THEATRE IN A MARKET-PLACE, Brussels, *c.* 1660. Painting by Adam van der Meulen

This painting shows excellently a well-developed form of the perennial street theatre. Note the blank central space and the two side entrances, reminiscent of the Swan.

The striped curtain is interesting: there are striped curtains mentioned for an English theatrical occasion as early as 1530, and striped curtains may be seen in the 1660 engraving for *The Wits* (see p. 30). The figure peeping over the curtain on the left reminds one of *Volpone*, v. i, where Volpone watches the reading of his will to his expectant (and disappointed) heirs:

> I'll get up
> Behind the curtain, on a stool, and hearken,
> Sometimes peep over, see how they do look . . .

which later he does (the stage direction says he *peepes from behind a traverse*), making asides during the scene. Note the height of the stage.

*Photo: Wolfrum, Vienna*

### 22. A MOUNTEBANK STAGE, *c.* 1600

An outdoor stage in its most primitive form, the nucleus and beginning of all stages. Note the height of it, which is characteristic. The actors are Italian Comedians, selling medicines (shown on the table at left). Again, as in Plate 21, one is reminded of *Volpone*, II. i, when, *disguised as a mountebank Doctor*, Volpone 'mounts his bank' under Celia's window, the 'bank' having been brought in and erected on the stage.

*British Museum*

### 23. A STREET THEATRE IN LOUVAIN, 1594

Primitive forms of street booth stages are shown in Plates 28 and 29, and in the text on pp. 32, 33. The booth here is interesting because it shows the next stage of development, i.e. ornamentation by painted fasciae. Note trestles.

This drawing is a nineteenth-century lithographic copy (by Edward van Even) of a sixteenth-century drawing which was destroyed in the burning of Louvain library in 1914. George R. Kernodle, from whose book *From Art to Theatre* this is taken, informs me that the buildings in the background were added by van Even, who says there was no background to the original which he copied.

The play appears to be a Judgement of Solomon.

*Kernodle:* From Art to Theatre

### 24. CHRIST SHOWN TO THE PEOPLE. Etching (1st state) by Rembrandt, 1655

There is good reason to suppose that this composition by Rembrandt is based upon a theatrical show seen and sketched by him in a Flemish street. The central structure has a marked resemblance to the *Rederyker* stages of the type shown in Plates 27, 32, and 33: the empty space on the upper level was probably originally an upper stage covered with a curtain. With a little imagination it is possible to see in this picture something of the appearance of a play in an Elizabethan inn-yard, or even perhaps something suggestive of a performance in Henslowe's square-built Fortune (though the stage of the Fortune was much larger).

*British Museum*

## 25. STAGE IN BRUSSELS, 1594

A Throne of Honour, attended by Virtues and Angels of Fame. The Virgin Mary descending from the Heavens in a Glory, or cloud-machine. The two-storey pavilion-type building at centre may be compared with the central feature at the Amsterdam Schouwburg (Plate 54) and perhaps with the *Messallina* tiring-house (Plate 49), which appears to be standing forward like this. See also the 'Theatrum Orbi' (Plate 18). Modern conjectures along the same lines are at Plates 11 and 71, and on p. 55.

*Kernodle:* From Art to Theatre

## 26. THE TARQUIN STAGE, AMSTERDAM, 1609

The occasion of this show, which was given in Amsterdam on 5 May 1609, by the Love-in-Bloom Rhetoric (*Rederyker*) Society, was the signing in the previous month of the Twelve Years' Truce which ended the long Dutch war with Spain. The appropriate subject chosen for this performance was the expulsion of the Tarquins from Rome. This record of it was engraved by J. C. Visscher after a drawing by Verschuring, and is quite unique as a record of any theatrical entertainment of the time, since the staging of each incident is shown in detail. There is one important factor, however, in which it differs from the more typical theatres of its period: it is a picture-frame stage. The reason for this is that it was not a play in the usual sense, but rather a series of short posed episodes, *tableaux vivants*, linked, presumably, by a descriptive recitation from the man who appears before the curtain in the central panel of the engraving. That the show was given in *tableau vivant* style is demonstrated not only by the picture-frame form of the stage itself, which we have just noted, but also by the staging of episode 9, in the bottom left corner. Obviously this episode can only have been staged by the use of one or perhaps two dummies, and the possibility of live action (if there was any action at all) was limited to the short time required for the striking off of two dummy heads, followed perhaps by some moralizing upon the general effect. The *tableau vivant* idea is also supported by the fact that in several of the views the hands of the curtain-drawers can be seen, which with the temporary way in which the curtains appear to be held back strongly suggests that each episode was only shown for a short while. In character and action the whole performance recalls the dumb shows of Elizabethan drama.

The episodes, which read always from left to right across the spread, are as follows: (1) Tarquin is shown in the symbolical action of striking down the tallest flowers of the land. (2) Another symbolic group which shows Tarquin treading the nobility of Rome under foot. Brutus, however, raises his head. (3) The Roman nobles visit the Delphic oracle who pronounces that he among them who first kisses his own mother shall be the deliverer of Rome from the tyrant. Brutus at once kisses Mother Earth. (4) Meanwhile Sextus, son of Tarquin, violates Lucretia, wife of Collatinus. (5) Lucretia announces her intention of wiping out the stain on her honour by killing herself. (This certainly suggests a speech by Lucretia.) (6) Lucretia stabs herself. Brutus and Collatinus vow vengeance. (7) The Tarquins are driven out. (8) The two sons of Brutus plot with Tarquin and Sextus to restore them to the kingdom. Note how simple is the method adopted to show the eavesdropper, through whom the plot is reported to Brutus. (9) Brutus, putting the security of the State above family, orders the execution of his sons. On the English stage at this time the actors would not have spared pains to make a dummy which would spurt real blood. Maybe the same was done in this case. (10) The freedom of the new Roman Republic, like the month-old Dutch Republic of 1609, is established and guarded by its heroes.

*From* Monumenta Scenica

## 27. FLEMISH STREET THEATRE, 1607

Note trestles supporting the stage.

*Photo: Oskar Fischel Collection*

## 28. BASQUE FOLK-DANCE STAGE, *c.* 1934

This stage, photographed by the late Rodney Gallop at Tardets in the Pyrenees, shows an ancient and traditional form of theatre still in use. Note especially (and compare with Plate 27 above) the trestled stage, the curtained booth, and the centrally placed upper stage which is occupied by musicians.

The dance here in progress was described by Rodney Gallop (in the *Geographical Magazine* for July 1935) as being dramatic in form, the action taking place between 'Christians' and 'Turks'. The Christians hold the stage, and some of the Turks are on horseback in front of it.

The following extract will also be of interest. It is from 'The Place of Rhythm in the Basque Pastorales' by Violet Alsford (*Journal of the English Folk Dance and Song Society*, Vol. VII, No. 1, December 1952):

The village people go to great expense when they decide to perform their play. The stage is of planks laid on barrels,[1] towering tiers of wooden seats are built up. . . . The backcloth is of beautifully-arranged white sheets lightly decorated in the tasteful manner of this people, with small green garlands swaying in the spring air. The traditional *tchirulari*, playing the three-holed pipe and the long, stringed drum, sits at the back of the stage. Other musicians (clarinet, brass, small drum) sit in an arbour constructed high above the backcloth. Below, two doors lead *on* to, not off from the stage and when actors enter, in the language

[1] Cf. Plate 19.

of the theatre, they 'go out' in the language of the Pastorale. This arrangement comes directly from the 'mansions' of the Mystery plays. Over the left-hand door are blue flowers, over the right-hand one red, and an Idol or Mahoma is fixed above the red one. This is a polichinelle figure with horns, partaking of the Devil and the supposed God of the Moors. . . . Sometimes there is a central door of gold and white for the use of Angels, Bishops, the lesser clergy, and the dead who enter Paradise through it.

The 'ladies' follow the fashion in their costumes and have done so for at least eighty years since they were in crinolines. In 1951 the Bride of Robert le Diable wore an elegant white dress made by the village dress-maker, with a wreath and veil from the Bon Marché of Bayonne. . .

*Photo: Paul Popper*

## 29. STREET THEATRE AND STROLLING PLAYERS, 1676

It was betwixt five and six of the clock, when a cart came into the market-place of Le Mans. This cart was drawn by two yoke of lean oxen, led by a breeding mare, who had a colt that skipped to and fro like a silly creature as he was. The cart was laden with trunks, portmanteaus, and great packs of painted clothes, that made a sort of pyramid, on top of which sat a damsel, in a half-city, half-country dress. A young man, as poor in clothes as rich in mien, walked by the side of the cart: he had a great patch on his face (which covered one of his eyes and half of one cheek) and carried a long birding-piece on his shoulder, wherewith he had murdered several magpies, jays and crows, which having strung together made him a sort of bandolier; at the bottom of which hung a hen and goose, that looked as if they had been taken from the enemy by way of plunder. Instead of a hat he wore a nightcap, tied about his head with garters of several colours, and which was without doubt a kind of unfinished turban. His doublet was a griset-coat, girt about with a leather thong, which served likewise to support a rapier so very long, that it could not be used dextrously without the help of a rest. He wore a pair of breeches tucked up to above the middle of his thigh, like those that players have when they represent an ancient hero. Instead of shoes he wore tragic buskins, bespattered with dirt up to the ankles. An old man, something more regular in his dress, though in very ordinary habit, walked by his side. He carried a bass viol on his shoulders; and because he stooped a little as he went, one might have taken him at a distance for a great tortoise walking upon its hind feet.

So begins the first chapter of the English translation of Scarron's *Comical Romance of a Company of Stage Players*, and it will be seen that the engraver of this title-page has not felt the need to read very far into the text for his subject. Had he done so he would have found that nowhere in the book do the players act on street stages as here shown, but always in inns or tennis courts. The first edition of the novel in France in 1651 had, so I now read, 'an engraved title page with Italian masquers on it'. I guess that this maybe is the same plate, or else is derived from it, and I therefore ought not to have said in the first edition of the present book that the picture shows an English street theatre.

*Photo: Common Ground Ltd.*

## *Section III. Pageants and Celebrations*

### 30 and 31. TWO DETAILS FROM 'THE TRIUMPH OF ISABELLA', 1615

The large painting by Denis van Alsloot from which these two details were taken is in the Victoria and Albert Museum, London, and shows a procession of ten splendid cars in the Baroque style winding through the Grande Place in Brussels. The procession was an annual one, but on the occasion shown here it was given with particular splendour in honour of the Archduchess Isabella of the Netherlands, who had distinguished herself a few days previously with the crossbow at a ceremonial shooting match given by the Guild of Crossbowmen, the senior Guild in charge of this procession. The Archduchess herself rode in the procession, and hers is the car shown in the foreground of Plate 31. She is attended by the ladies of her court, and Fame sits before her on a pillar, sounding upon two trumpets (cf. also Plate 50). Other cars partly seen in the background carry tableaux of the Annunciation (left) and the Stem of Jesse (right). The principal car in Plate 30 presents a tableau of the Nativity, attended by peasants. In the background is one of a fantastic file of processional monsters.

I include these pictures within my subject principally to show the rich style in which an essentially theatrical display was decorated at that time. Note especially the fine painted hangings. In the Nativity group it is of interest to note how elaborate Corinthian columns have been combined with a thatched roof. If the stage roof at the First Globe was thatched (like the rest of that theatre), it might be supposed to have been supported on similar columns (as in the Swan drawing, q.v.) and the effect would have been something like we see here.

*Victoria and Albert Museum*

### 32. *REDERYKER* STAGE AT ANTWERP, 1582

One of a series erected for the ceremonial welcome of Francis of Anjou, Duke of Brabant. Others of this series of stages were built to a similar pattern, having like this one a large upper stage on which biblical tableaux were presented and a lower stage enclosing an allegorical figure: in this instance a Fury or Vice is seen locked in the dungeon of Hell.

*From* Monumenta Scenica

### 33. STREET THEATRE, GHENT, 1539

Another example of the ornate *Rederyker* stage. It will be observed that this florid Baroque style of theatre architecture was well established in the Netherlands as early as 1539.

### 34. THE TRIUMPH OF JAMES I, LONDON, 1604: (1) The Flemish Arch

That many of the foregoing examples are Flemish and not English may be argued against their acceptance as evidence for the style of the Elizabethan theatre. But our next six examples, which were built in the streets of London for the coronation procession of James I, are English; and if they are not strictly theatres, they are theatrical in their character, construction, and use. This and its neighbour may be compared with the two Flemish examples opposite, and it will be seen that there is nothing to choose between them in point of style and ornament. As a useful link between the English and Flemish examples, this (Plate 34) shows the Flemish offering to the London celebrations. It features James I in his Imperial robes. Beneath him are figures representing the seventeen provinces of Flanders. Other figures represent political emblems. Surmounting the whole is a figure of Divine Providence.

*British Museum*

## 35. THE TRIUMPH OF JAMES I, 1604: (2) The Temple of Janus

The theme of this arch, which stood at Temple Bar, was devised by Ben Jonson. Its central feature, immediately over the arch, was a tableau in which a figure representing the Genius of the City of London (right), after a dialogue with a Roman Flamen, sacrificed the heart of the City to James. The part of the Genius of the City was spoken by the actor Edward Alleyn. In the niche above is the figure of Peace, with War grovelling at her feet. The other niches hold figures of Quiet, Safety, Felicity, and Liberty, trampling upon Tumult, Danger, Unhappiness, and Servitude respectively.

The engravings of all this series of triumphal arches were made by Kip under the supervision of the designer and builder of them, Stephen Harrison. Harrison tells us, in his accompanying description, that the walls and gates of this arch were made to resemble brass, the pillars silver, with bases and capitals of gold.

*British Museum*

## 36. THE TRIUMPH OF JAMES I, 1604: (3) The Arch of London

This arch, devised by Ben Jonson, stood in Fenchurch Street, where James began his procession. As he approached, a silk curtain painted to represent a cloud, which was spread across the top part of the arch, dropped, and revealed the panorama of London which we see here. At the same time the 'waites and hault-boyes of the City', seen in the openings on each side, began to play, and the Genius of the City (personified by Edward Alleyn) began his speech of welcome. He is seen in the central niche, his arm raised. On either side of him stand figures of the Wisdom and Warlike Strength of the City. Above him, on the highest throne, sits Monarchia Britannia, with, on the lesser thrones beneath her, Gladness, Loving Affection, Unanimity, Promptitude, and Vigilance. The Genius of the City rouses old Thames, who is shown asleep on the pedestal below, and he also speaks his welcome before the King passes through on his way to the next arch.

*British Museum*

## 37. THE TRIUMPH OF JAMES I: (4) The Garden of Plenty

This magnificent arbour, at which the King arrived midway in his procession and where he stopped to refresh himself, 'seemed to grow' close to the little Conduit in Cheapside, which 'served as a Fountain to water the Fruits of Plenty. . . . The roof and sides of these Gates were hung with Pompions, Cowcumbers, Grapes, Cherries, Peares, Apples and all other fruits which the land bringeth forth.' The round tops were 'garnished with lesser fruits and all sorts of flowers made by Art'. On the summit of the structure stood Fortune. In the niche below were Peace and Plenty; and below them again Gold and Silver supporting the Globe of the World, with Pomona and Ceres on each side. In the openings above the archways sat the Nine Muses (left) and the Seven Liberal Sciences (right). The King, as he approached, was met by 'Sylvanus and his followers, who, upon sight of his Majesty played upon Cornets' and escorted him to a room above, where refreshment awaited him.

*British Museum*

## 38. THE TRIUMPH OF JAMES I, 1604: (5) The New Arabia Felix

Thomas Dekker was responsible for this conception. The Arabia Felix of the title signified the happy land of Britain. As James drew near, Fame, in the topmost alcove, blew her trumpet, whereupon the personages in the large opening below awoke as from sleep and the fountain in the centre (The Fount of Virtue) 'ran wine very plenteously'. The figures of the display represented the Five Senses 'upon five green mounts', with, reclining in the foreground, Oblivion and Detraction. These, when the trumpet wakened them, tried to break down the Fount of Virtue with clubs, but the Five Senses prevented them. Once again, as in Plate 36, we see the musicians in the galleries at the sides.

Thirty feet in front of this arch there was a stage set up, 'railed round about with pilasters', upon which verses were recited by a number of allegorical personages.

*British Museum*

## 39. THE TRIUMPH OF JAMES I, 1604: (6) The Arch of the New World

In the centre of this Baroque fantasy (for which Thomas Middleton was in part responsible) is a great Globe 'filled with all the estates that are in the land'. Upon it stands Fortune, and around it stand the Four Elements, Fire, Air, Earth, and Water, who keep it turning like a wheel. Harrison says the Elements 'were placed so quaintly that the Globe seemed to have his motion even on the Crowns of their heads'. Among the twenty-three figures of this display, described as 'lively garnishments' were The Four Cardinal Virtues (Justice, Fortitude, Temperance, and Prudence) enclosed on the (spectator's) right of the Globe, and the four Kingdoms of England,

Scotland, Ireland, and France, on the left. Perhaps in this case only the Four Elements were living persons, the rest being either paintings or effigies.

*British Museum*

### 40. THE CHARIOT OF ROYAL JUSTICE

An engraving of the early seventeenth century (from a drawing by Martin de Vos) which illustrates not only the design of a processional car, with an outdoor stage (in background), but also the fashionable taste in allegory. A king, attended by Wisdom and Justice, is drawn by the two horses of Rewards and Punishments—these being the theme also represented by the tableaux on the stage.

### 41. THE ELVETHAM ENTERTAINMENT FOR QUEEN ELIZABETH I, 1591

An eighteenth-century engraving copied from a contemporary original. The Queen was entertained at Elvetham, in Hampshire, by the Earl of Hertford. For the spectacle shown here this crescent-shaped lake had been specially made, and, because his own house was too small for the Queen and her Court, he had built a state room and other buildings for her in the park. These are shown at the top of the picture.

In the lake were a 'Ship Isle' (D), whose masts turned into trees (presumably the three flagged columns in this engraving represent the masts); a Fort, given by Neptune for the protection of the Queen; and a 'Snail Mount' (G), which, although it is not clear from this picture how it did so, was supposed at one point to represent the Armada, in the guise of a monster with horns of wild-fire. Upon the lake floated a pinnace, a gift from 'gold-breasted India' to the Queen, which with a nymph and her maidens in it singing was drawn across the lake by Neptune and his attendants 'with grisly heads and beards of divers colours and fashions', to where Elizabeth sat enthroned at the water's edge at the western shore of the pond. Commentators have seen in this famous occasion some possibility that Shakespeare may have had it in mind when he was writing Oberon's speech in *A Midsummer Night's Dream*, about the 'fair Vestal throned by the West'.

*From Nichol's* Progresses of Queen Elizabeth

### 42. FESTIVAL CAR AND COSTUMES, BRUNSWICK, 1616

*Photo: Oskar Fischel Collection*

### 43. BIOSCOPE ORGAN, ANTWERP, c. 1910

In this façade from a Flemish fair-ground one may see a last survivor of the baroque festival architecture shown in the preceding pages. A glance between them will show the similarity of effect, the identity of intention. Here is a true descendant of the theatrical 'Venus palaces' that shocked the Puritans in Elizabethan London.

In her book *The Unsophisticated Arts* Barbara Jones says of this and other such fair-ground organs that they 'were made for dance halls on the Continent, where they stood at one end and provided the music, or for Bioscope shows (early travelling cinemas). When the popularity of the Bioscope declined, the organs were used for other purposes [e.g. roundabouts].' This example may be estimated as about 20 feet high, to the apex.

*Barbara Jones Collection*

## 44. STAGING AT COURT, 1581

The method of the dispersed or simultaneous setting commonly used for courtly entertainments, before it was superseded by the Italian invention of the integrated perspective setting, is here illustrated in the frontispiece to the account published in 1582 of Balthasar de Beaujoyeux's 'Ballet Comique de la Reine', which was performed in the Salle du Petit-Bourbon, Paris.

The settings are: in the background a triple arbour, with the Garden of Circe before it, full of beasts; seen through the arbour is Circe's palace, presumably painted on a cloth; near the Garden stands an ornate fountain; forward on the left is a sort of Heaven, formed like an arcaded enclosure made of star-spangled clouds, and facing it on the other side of the floor is a Grove of Pan.

*British Museum*

## Section IV. Costumes and Indoor Theatres

## 45. A SCENE FROM *TITUS ANDRONICUS*, c. 1595

This contemporary drawing is ascribed to the hand of Henry Peacham, author of *The Complete Gentleman*, and is generally believed to date from about 1594 or 1595, that is, more or less contemporary with the de Witt sketch of the Swan theatre. In this connection Professor J. Dover Wilson has something to say[1] regarding the respective merits of the two drawings. 'I would point', he says, 'to the elaborate hypothetical structures that have been erected from the material furnished by one Dutchman's copy of another Dutchman's sketch of what he remembered about the interior of the Swan theatre after a single visit, and ask whether speculations based upon this [*Titus Andronicus*] much neglected, unique and finished drawing of Shakespeare's fellows in action on his stage and performing one of the plays of his canon, may not be more profitable.'

What concerns us here is the contemporary record of the costumes worn. They comprise a mixture of contemporary dress (for the lesser characters) and an attempt at Roman dress for the principals. A comparison with the costumes in the Tarquin

[1] *Shakespeare Survey 1*, 1948.

play (Plate 26) shows an interesting similarity, especially in the case of Aaron's tunic, made in the style of Roman armour, but (as can be clearly seen in the Tarquin pictures) of fabric or leather. The treatment of Aaron as a coal-black blackamoor gives rise to speculation about the usual way of representing Moors on the Elizabethan stage, with of course its implication for Othello.

The use of scarves knotted on the shoulder should be noted.

*Reproduced by permission of the Marquess of Bath, Longleat*

### 46. COSTUMES IN THE ROMAN STYLE, *c.* 1611

These figures of Boadicea and Petillius Cerealis do not come from a theatrical source, but are part of the ornament of a Jacobean map of Essex. It will be seen, however, that they are entirely in accord with the theatrical dresses shown in Plate 45. They are also similar to many of the theatrical designs of Inigo Jones (cf. Plate 68a).

This and the following plate are taken from John Speed's atlas, *The Theatre of the Empire of Great Britain.* The engravings are by Jodocus Hondius, a Fleming, but the work was devised and published in England. The first edition appeared in 1611, but loose plates were in circulation at an earlier date, and the style of costume and decoration throughout the book may be accepted as a true reflection of the style which would have been considered correct in the theatre during Shakespeare's hey-day.

*British Museum*

### 47. JOHN SPEED'S TITLE-PAGE, 1614

It ought, perhaps, to be made clear that the word 'theatre' in this title is strictly a coincidence: here it means only 'a scene of action' in a general sense, for the book is an atlas. However, it may be seen that the whole arrangement and detail of this delightful composition is in fact theatrical in character and corresponds entirely with what we have already seen of the style of the Flemish theatres and the English triumphal arches. Apart from this, there is a special interest in the figures shown here, for they are all labelled with the periods for which they are supposed to be historically representative, and there are in fact many attempts at historical accuracy, e.g. the top figure of a 'Britaine', moustachioed and woaded. At bottom right the 'Norman' is represented as wearing pointed medieval shoes—a deliberate historical archaism. But for the most part the historical element is fanciful and theatrical: the open robe of the 'Saxon', for instance, may be compared with the robes of the dramatic figures in Plate 48.

It is reasonable to suppose that this engraving would have been familiar to Shakespeare and his fellows, and it would be almost *un*reasonable to think that their own choice of costumes would not have been influenced by such pictures.

*British Museum*

## 48. BEN JONSON'S TITLE-PAGE, 1616

It should first be noted that this engraving is from the hand not of a Flemish but of an English engraver, William Hole. It is also not improbable that Jonson himself may have had a hand in laying out the details of the design, especially in its classical allusions.

The figures represent Tragedy and Comedy, and (top) Tragi-Comedy, dressed in a half-and-half mixture of the style of the other two; the remaining large figures represent satirical and pastoral drama. Above the title panel is a Jacobean (Jonson's?) idea of a Roman theatre, and at the foot of the page are two little panels representing what was then known of the Greek theatre: on the right an amphitheatre with a Chorus around the altar; on the left Thespis in his cart (but very much obscured!), to which is tethered the goat (*Tragos*) from which the word 'tragedy' is derived.

*British Museum*

## 49 and 50. THE *MESSALLINA* AND *ROXANA* TITLE-PAGES

These two small engravings (here reproduced slightly larger than original size) are important as showing, each in the centre bottom panel, the only known pictures of *English* stages of Shakespearian or quasi-Shakespearian type, other than the Swan drawing and the *Wits* frontispiece. Even so, they are a late reference and their derivation is unsure. They are presumed by some authorities to represent college performances. Both show a background of hangings (the *Messallina* has tapestry) and a wedge-shaped stage with a railing. Except for the central upper opening of the *Messallina* stage, they could, and indeed might, be the same place.

Of the two the *Roxana* is by far the better engraving. The classical/dramatic costumes are worth noting, as also the figure of Fame, which may be compared with that in Plate 31.

*British Museum*

## 51. THE MERMAID THEATRE, LONDON, 1951

This stage was designed for Bernard Miles by Michael Stringer and the author. It was intended as a free experiment in the Elizabethan style, and not as a reconstruction in the antiquarian sense. It was used with success for productions not only of Elizabethan drama, but of Restoration opera. It is included here in order that something of the effect of the ornate style can be seen in living terms, as compared with the engravings on other pages.

This stage was used for two seasons. Subsequently a new Mermaid Theatre was built and now stands on Thames-side, 100 yards from the site of the old Blackfriars Playhouse, and within view of the site of the Globe across the river.

*Photo: Millar and Harris*

## 52, 53, 54. THE SCHOUWBURG, AMSTERDAM, 1658. Engraving by S. Savry

Before the 'scenery theatre' with its proscenium frame had established itself as the pattern for all future theatre building in Europe, there were one or two attempts made in the mid-seventeenth century to establish a development of the old and traditional actors' stage in a permanent indoor setting. One such theatre was Shakespeare's Blackfriars (1608–55), of which no stage details are known. Another was Jacob van Campen's theatre in Amsterdam, the subject of these three engravings. This appears to have been a complete hybrid, having not only some of the qualities of dispersed setting in the medieval style, with a King's throne in the centre and a Heavens gallery above it, but also a rudimentary provision for painted wings, which could be changeable, set between the pillars at the sides. There is also a curtain provided, which can be hung across the stage, leaving only a narrow apron in front of it, but this would seem to have been awkwardly managed—leastwise, if the arrangement shown in Plate 54 was the usual one. In accordance with a practice commonly found at this period, the curtain was a striped one.

The wide, shallow layout of the auditorium is more related to the proportion of the Elizabethan theatre yard than to the horseshoe layout of proscenium theatres. The Elizabethan touch and the derivation from the popular street theatre is given also by the fact that the floor space was for standing spectators, and that the stage, as can be judged by comparing the level of the lower boxes with the figure coming in at the door in Plate 52, was high.

*Richard Southern Collection*

## 55. DESIGN FOR THE COCKPIT-IN-COURT THEATRE, LONDON, c. 1632

The little Cockpit at Whitehall Palace had been in occasional use as a theatre ever since the time of James I. In 1632 it appears to have been rebuilt as a theatre only, and this design, possibly from the hand of Inigo Jones, may have been made with that reconstruction in mind. On the other hand the drawing may have to do with a later restoration of the Cockpit in 1660, for the return of Charles II. William Grant Keith (*Architectural Review*, February 1925) has given reason to think that the design is not by Inigo Jones but by his nephew and disciple John Webb, which would bring it nearer to the later date.

The drawing as it stands is full of puzzles, more like a project in the half-way stage of working-out than a finished design. For example, the direction of ascent of the flight of stairs at the bottom of the plan (right) is ambiguous, and whichever way they go it will be seen that we are in doubt about which level, up or down, the plan chiefly shows. Mostly the ground level, we may presume. Then there is a (presumably) foot scale, just discernible, marked along the bottom of the paper. Estimates of the size of the stage, made from this, show it to be $4\frac{1}{2}$ feet high, 35 feet wide and 16 feet deep. But it shows also that except for the central arch all the doors on to the stage are only 5 feet high. This is so improbable that it must mean either that the scale is not meant to apply to this drawing, but to some other on another piece of

The Cockpit-in-Court: a conjectural reconstruction

paper, or that the designer's ideas had changed since the scale was drawn. Further, one may be in doubt as to the meaning of the two angled walls of masonry within the auditorium, against the stage. Clearly they are set at a different level from the stage, since they do not appear in the larger plan of this. Clearly, also, they cannot be solid walls. However, they do occupy the position where one may suppose it necessary to have a support for the roof, and it may therefore be assumed that this part of the drawing represents a masonry foundation upon which stood vertical members supporting the roof, perhaps a collonade of tall pillars or (in every way more likely) a framework including a gallery. The rough sketch given on page 134 is based upon the latter assumption, and, if correct, would help to decide the puzzle of the stairs, mentioned above. There are twenty-one steps, just about the right number to take us from the lower gallery to an upper one about 11 or 12 feet overhead.

Whether or not the Cockpit-in-Court was ever built at all like this, the design itself has value as a theatrical concept, since it shows how the old classical idea of a theatre lingered on far into the seventeenth century, as being the only proper theatrical form, in spite of all the then recent innovations of scenery and proscenium arches. In Restoration times Sir Christopher Wren, before he emerged with his proscenium-style Drury Lane, was still contemplating a public theatre in this 'arena' form (cf. Nicoll, *Development of the Theatre*, figs. 192, 193). De Witt, as we have seen, believed the Swan to have been a revival in spirit of the theatres of ancient Rome. This Jones/Webb Cockpit, clearly influenced by Palladio's Roman-style theatre at Vicenza, and based upon the principles of Vitruvius, is merely a refinement of the same idea. Therefore, whether it was ever built or not, this design may be taken as a final glow of light from the ideas that once guided the building of the Globe.

*Worcester College Library, Oxford*

## Section V. Tricks and Machines

### 56. FURTENBACH'S THEATRICAL EFFECTS, 1663

Joseph Furtenbach, the author of the *Mannhafter Kunstspiegel*, a work on scenic technique from which these engravings are taken, was born in 1591, and travelled in Italy between 1612 and 1622. Thus his book, which was published in Augsburg when Furtenbach was 72, fairly represents the stage fashions of the first half of the seventeenth century. Although he is primarily concerned with proscenium-stage effects, many of the devices shown on this page are of a traditional character. If there had been illustrations to Philip Henslowe's property list given on p. 72, they would not have looked very different from this. The items are as follows (I shall refer to each row by the letter in the margin and each picture by its number in the row, from left to right):

*Row A*: Celestial effects. A1 is described by Furtenbach as 'a box 5 feet square and 4½ feet deep, with a back seat and two side seats for three angels, little boys dressed in white with red sashes and curly wigs. The inside of the box is covered with brass or gilt in a rough manner, so as to catch and reflect the light. Candles put inside, but carefully shaded. The outside is painted with angels' heads. The whole is lowered by a windlass arrangement and appears between other clouds.' No. A4 in the row shows a gilded box with an opening at back which is covered with a shutter, as shown in A3. The shutter is painted with clouds, but behind it is placed a glass of water with a light at the back, which shines out when the shutter is opened. Other shaded lights are placed at 'pp' and 'oo' in A4. A2 shows the complete arrangement. 'The sun in this', says Furtenbach, 'is made of brass . . . and polished with brick dust. The eye in the middle O is cut out, and an uneven glass flask filled with coloured water fixed into the hole, through which the light will shine in broken colours. By an arrangement of rods this eye can be turned, and can thus shine and twinkle more. When God or Moses speaks, the whole sun is turned round.'

*Row B.* B1 is a counterweighted crane for lowering a painted cloud from the Heavens. An angel seated in the middle 'steps out when the cloud is lowered, fulfils his office, and is taken up again by the cloud'. B2 is a variation of B1. The angel sits between the painted clouds at the point marked RR. B3 is a device in a play about Jonah: the prophet watches the fruit grow and decay before his eyes. The fruit is painted green on one side and rotting on the other, and the effect is gained simply by having it mechanically turned round. B4 is a throne for Pharaoh.

*Row C.* C1 shows three kinds of waves for sea effects. The top one is a cut-out ground row, to stand against a backcloth. The middle one represents 'moving sea-waves; these are painted in a more lively style, pushed backwards and forwards on a rail'. At the bottom are 'very great waves; they have to be painted on fin-like protrusions and fixed with nails into a big wooden pole, which can be turned on the pivots yy like a spit'. C2 are also waves, but they are used 'for the passage of the Israelites through the Red Sea, and are put right and left into the floor, with a counterweight and rods attached to them at b, so that they can be lowered gradually in order to drown Pharaoh . . .'. C3 is a painted rock, apparently with a pedestal at the top; perhaps intended for Moses on Mount Sinai.

*Row D.* D1: Jonah's Whale. 'It has globes and lights in its eyes, a hole on the far side by which Jonah can escape below the scene and rest until it is time for him to creep back into the fish and be spat out again. The whale can be raised and lowered on a hinge. . . . Its jaw is opened by a wire or string from above, and is weighted so that it closes over Jonah of its own accord when the wire is slackened.' D2: a boat to be moved along behind the waves (C1). It is pulled by cords at yy, and can be made to rock on a pivot. D3 is a device for the burning bush in the Moses play referred to above (C2 and C3). The parasol framework, decorated like a bush painted in gold, is hidden among naturally painted bushes. At the proper moment it is opened from below by invisible means and, with lamps shining upon it, appears to burn.

*Oskar Fischel Collection*

57. INIGO JONES: A FANTASTIC ELEPHANT

*The Trustees of the Chatsworth Settlement*

## 58. THE NORWICH DRAGON

Snap the Dragon was a traditional feature of municipal pageantry in Norwich until the Reform of the Municipal Corporations in 1835. There are three versions of Snap at the Castle Museum, Norwich, all varying a little in detail. The one shown in this illustration is the oldest, and belongs to the eighteenth century. The idea, however, is considered to date back to the Middle Ages, and therefore may fairly be offered as an example of a popular theatrical device familiar in Elizabethan times. The effigy was carried on a harness over the shoulders of a man whose head poked out of the hole seen in the middle of the back, and whose legs were hidden by the skirt below. The carved wooden head is attached to a short pole which enabled the carrier to move it backwards and forwards and also to a limited extent from side to side. The jaws were raised and lowered by means of a string. The carved wooden wings are fixed. The body is coloured green, and the scales are outlined in gold.

*Photo: A. E. Coe & Sons, Norwich*
*Reproduced by permission of the Norwich Museums Committee*

## 59. MECHANICAL DEVILS, FIFTEENTH CENTURY

Among the scenes in Marlowe's *Doctor Faustus* which have been interpolated (probably by another hand) from the stock-in-trade of the medieval theatre there is one in which Faustus bids Mephistophilis fetch him a wife. Mephistophilis is reluctant, but then agrees, as follows:

MEPH. Well, wilt thou have one? Sit there till I come. I'll fetch thee a wife in the devil's
name.                                                                                              [*Exit.*
*Re-enter* MEPHISTOPHILIS *with a* DEVIL *drest like a Woman, with fireworks.*
MEPH. Tell me, Faustus, how dost thou like thy wife?
FAUST. A plague on her for a hot whore!

The long tradition behind this joke is well illustrated by the first of the four drawings here reproduced, from an Italian MS. belonging to the first half of the fifteenth century. It shows a mechanical figure of a woman mounted on an armature (shown in detail on her right) who at an appropriate moment turns into a devil. Her bat's wings are at first hanging down at her side, so that they resemble the long sleeves of a fashionable dress; her horns are concealed behind her head-dress. But at the pull of a string the wings and horns swivel round on a pivot and stand upright. At the same time the fireworks start blazing from her mouth and ears.

The second picture on this page shows a moving effigy of a great devil made up of articulated parts, some of which are shown in the sketches below. The devil is enthroned upon a furnace.

*Bavarian State Library, Munich*

## 60. THEATRICAL FLYING APPARATUS, SEVENTEENTH CENTURY

This drawing shows a system of winding-drums, counterweights, and escapements for a flying throne and for the free flight of a Mercury and cupids. The hoisting gear can be moved to any position along the joists which support them. The three frames marked RRR may represent traps from which the cupids can fly up from under the stage, or perhaps screens from behind which the lines can be attached to the flyers unnoticed, when required.

The drawing is one of a series which Edward Carrick (*Architectural Review*, August 1931) attributes to the Mauro brothers, and which may have been copied from the work of the famous Giacomo Torelli at a theatre in Venice between 1640 and 1645. However, the apparatus shown here is applicable to the ordinary Elizabethan theatre. Cranford Adams considers that the technique of free flying was first introduced on the London stage with Ariel in *The Tempest*. The flying throne, on the other hand, is a device which dates back at least as far as 1587, when Greene specifies the use of one in his play *Alphonsus, King of Aragon*.

*Palatine Library, Parma*

## 61. A JACOBEAN 'HEAVENS' AT CULLEN HOUSE, BANFFSHIRE

This ceiling is preserved in its original paint at Cullen House, Banffshire, and is believed to date from the first decade of the seventeenth century. Its relevance to the present subject is discussed in Chapter 5, p. 69. Although Oliver Hill thinks this work may be attributed to Flemish artists, he says in his book on Scottish castles that the London painter Valentine Jenking, with his assistant Andrew Horne and one Matthew Guidrick (Goodrich?) were fetched to Scotland to decorate Holyrood House for King James VI. So the Flemings did not have it all. Valentine Jenking may have gone on to Cullen. And what one wonders, had he painted when in London?

*Photo:* Country Life

## 62. THE TROJAN WAR AT CULLEN HOUSE

> At last she calls to mind where hangs a piece
> Of skilful painting made for Priam's Troy;
> Before the which is drawn the power of Greece
> For Helen's rape the city to destroy,
> Threatening cloud-kissing Ilion with annoy;
>     Which the conceited painter drew so proud
>     As Heaven, it seemed, to kiss the turrets bow'd.
>         *The Rape of Lucrece*, ll. 1366–72

How skilful in fact was the conceited painter? What sort of painting of the siege and fall of Troy might Shakespeare and his friends have seen in their day? One suspects there could not have been many. Paintings of fine quality were rare, and most of these would not have been dramatic scenes, but family portraits, hanging in a very few wealthy houses. Any paintings of the Trojan War that Shakespeare might have seen would most likely have been such as we see here, colourful, vernacular, and coarse.

Like the Heavens which adjoin this painting at Cullen House (Plate 61) it can be directly related to the Elizabethan stage. This is the kind of scene-painting that must have been used to depict the 'Cittie of Rome' listed in Henslowe's inventory. In the City of Troy shown here we see what Marlowe must have imagined for his topless towers of Ilium. They are labelled 'ILLON', to make no doubt of it; and over the gate the word 'TROA' is written. The gate-piece by itself might be a theatrical property straight from the tiring-house, and we are reminded at once of the 'Thebes written in great letters upon an old door' which Sir Philip Sydney derided. As for the Trojan Horse here depicted, we find it again in the Second Part of Heywood's *Iron Age*. In this play, in Act III, King Priam and the Trojans come out on to the stage as if wandering about amazed in the deserted Grecian camp-site. Then, says the stage direction, *The Horse is discovered*, meaning that it is revealed by the drawing of a curtain. The great size of the horse is commented on. There is a door in it, which later Synon unlocks, and *Pyrhus, Diomed and the rest leape from out the Horse, and, as if groping in the darke, meete with Agamemnon and the rest*. . . . Doubtless the horse was a large painting, perhaps cut out in profile, and it seems to have stood a long while on the stage, since in the next act Pyrhus speaks of 'yon Horse', and describes how he was the first to leap out of it. There has been another 'discovery' in the meantime, which seems to imply there were at least two curtained spaces available on this occasion at the Red Bull. The spectacular resources demanded by the two *Iron Age* plays were such that Heywood tells us that two companies of actors combined to perform them 'upon one Stage at once'; and they were so popular that they 'have at sundry times thronged three several Theatres with numerous and mighty Auditories . . .'.

In the painting the woman and child on the left are probably meant for Andromache and Astyanax. The combatants in the foreground may be Hector and Achilles, as Heywood, and perhaps Shakespeare also, would have imagined them.

*Photo:* Country Life

## Section VI. Masques

### 63. SIR HENRY UNTON'S WEDDING MASQUE, *c.* 1597

In its original form a masque represented the ceremonial visit with which some heroic or divine personage blessed a festive occasion. At an appropriate moment of the evening the Visitor would enter from the world outside, accompanied by his torch-bearers and musicians and by his knights, who would then lead out the ladies of their choice from among the company into the dance. This form still underlay all masquing in Shakespeare's time, though the addition of antimasques and of dialogue and songs specially composed by poets was gradually changing it into a more dramatic form. Enormous sums of money were frequently spent on these entertainments.

The portrait of Sir Henry Unton (1557–96), which was finished after his death, shows him seated in the midst of a progression of scenes representing the principal events of his life, with his death and burial. Prominent among these scenes is his wedding feast and masque, the portion here reproduced. Sir Henry is shown seated at the centre of the table, bare-headed. His wife is at the end on the right. The masquers have entered, led and presented by a green-clad huntsman who is seen addressing Lady Unton. The torchbearers are naked children, in pairs, black and white, perhaps representing the Cupids of Night and Day. The principal masquers are Mercury, with Diana and her huntresses in pairs, each carrying either a garland or a bow and arrows. The masquers are dressed in a silver-coloured stuff patterned over with sprays of green leaves, with red flowers. Their head-dresses are of silver, garlanded, and their faces are covered with masks of red. The long scarves which the children wear trailing from their heads are parti-coloured in red and white. At the right, half-hidden by the pillar, is a taborer. The procession is reminiscent of the nuptial procession of the fairies through the house of Theseus at the end of *A Midsummer Night's Dream*.

*National Portrait Gallery, London*

### 64. A LADY IN MASQUE COSTUME, *c.* 1610

The sumptuousness and extravagance which were lavished upon private dresses for court masques, and the craftsmanship which Inigo Jones could rely upon in the execution of his costume designs, may all be studied in this charming portrait, enlarged from a miniature by Isaac Oliver.

*Victoria and Albert Museum*

### 65. INIGO JONES: DRESS DESIGN FOR AN OCEANID AS TORCHBEARER. From the 'Masque of Blackness', 1605

*By permission of the Trustees of the Chatsworth Settlement*

### 66. INIGO JONES: DRESS DESIGN FOR IRIS. From the masque 'Hymenaei', 1606

*By permission of the Trustees of the Chatsworth Settlement*

### 67 and 68. INIGO JONES: DESIGNS FOR THE MASQUE OF 'OBERON', 1611

Inigo Jones (1573–1651), after studying painting and architecture in Italy, returned to England in 1605, where he was at once employed as architect and designer to Anne,

James I's Queen. His designs for Court masques were based upon the Italian style, and were of such inventive magnificence as eventually to incur the wrath of his collaborator, Ben Jonson, who held that this 'painting and carpentry' should not be allowed to usurp the admiration which more properly belonged to poetry, for which it was supposed to be only an adornment. That, however, refers particularly to the more elaborate masques of Charles I's reign. The designs reproduced here have all been chosen from those made in Jones's earliest period, during the lifetime of Shakespeare. The 'Oberon' series are the first extant examples in the history of the English theatre of scenery and costumes designed together for one play by the same artist. 'Oberon, the Faery Prince' was presented in the Banqueting House, Whitehall, on 1 January 1611, by Henry Frederick, Prince of Wales, who himself appeared as Oberon. The first scene showed a rocky cliff, in front of which the antimasque was performed by Satyrs. The cliff then opened and revealed the front of 'a bright and glorious *Palace*, whose gates and walls were transparent'. After some dancing, and at the crowing of a cock, this in its turn opened and revealed 'the nation of Faies', with Oberon in a chariot drawn by two white bears, and the knightly masquers ranked on seats around him. The principal dances of the masque then took place.

Plate 67 shows two of the scenes for this. At the bottom (right) is the rocky cliff of the antimasque. Above is the front of Oberon's palace. Below, left, is a detail sketch for part of this, upon the back of which Inigo Jones has noted down the dimensions: the 'heyght of the middell space' was 9 feet, and its breadth 5 feet; the height of the towers at the side, to the level of their battlements, was 11 feet; of the columns on the first storey, 7 feet; and of the 'terms', i.e. the caryatid-like figures carrying the pediment, 4 feet 1 inch. In both drawings the spaces for the transparency mentioned above can be seen.

Plate 68 gives some of the costumes for 'Oberon'. At top left is a 'Knight Masquer'. The others are all 'Faies'.

*By permission of the Trustees of the Chatsworth Settlement*

#### 69. BUILDING A PLAYHOUSE

This and the sketches which follow are intended to explore certain possibilities relating to the structure and form of the stage tiring-house. In this drawing we see the basic shape of the upper stage as a floor set within the chord of three bays of the house. In this instance it is stepped down a little below the level of the middle gallery. (The height of the house galleries need not necessarily control the heights of other things related to the stage.)

#### 70. A CURTAINED TIRING-HOUSE

If the open frame of the tiring-house in the preceding picture were simply to be hung with curtains, the effect produced would be as here. It makes a very practical shape of stage, which with modifications can be seen in action in Plate 73. However, it should be remembered that such an expanse of curtains hung in an open-air theatre would present a draught problem. The hangings would tend to suck and blow about uncontrollably every time an outer door was opened, unless there were a solid screening wall fairly close behind the hangings for most of their length. For this reason I am inclined to think that free-hanging curtains on Elizabethan public stages would not have been very large in area. (The hangings around the stage itself could, of course, be tied to the posts.)

## 71. TIRING-HOUSE: ORNATE STYLE

This sketch is an attempt to satisfy the idea that the tiring-house might have had a visual identity suitable for the temples and senate-houses so often referred to. Portia (*Merchant of Venice*, II. i) says to the Prince of Morocco, leading him back to the tiring-house at the end of the scene: 'First, forward to the temple.' What temple? Presumably a church is meant; but an ornate stage building in the Flemish *Rederyker* style might, for the eye, fill in the meaning of the word.

I had it particularly in mind, while making this sketch, to provide among other things a solution to the 'two windo's . . . of two contiguous buildings' which Ben Jonson specified for the scene with Wittipol and Mrs. Fitzdottrel in *The Devil Is An Ass* (cf. p. 61 above). I am aware that the arrangement in question was at the Black-friars and not at a public theatre, but, wherever it was, an arrangement like this would have served the purpose of the scene, if the two characters had acted at the two win-dows angled together at the side of the stage. I must admit, however, that a purely formal arrangement, out of two windows side by side as in the next picture, might possibly serve just as well.

## 72. TIRING-HOUSE: SCREEN STYLE

Basically this is the same as in the large drawing between pp. 90–91, and is a variant of the general solution I am most inclined to favour. The chief difference is that I have here supposed a big double-hung door in the centre, assuming that for discovery scenes a curtained booth could be stood in front of this where necessary, or the opening itself hung with curtains, the leaves of the door being opened back towards the inside. This sketch was made theoretically, before Bernheimer had published his discovery of Fludd's 'Theatrum Orbi' (Plate 18) which features the central door. I take Fludd's picture to be a useful corroboration.

Another point in this very rough sketch is the gutter which I have indicated around the 'shadow or cover' of the Heavens roof. Here I have supposed a tiled roof, as at the Fortune, where there was to be a gutter of lead 'to carry and convey the water from the covering of the said stage to fall backwards'. In the sketch the water runs back from the stage roof to a down-pipe in the angle between the tiring-house and the auditorium galleries. It falls thence to a gutter round the perimeter of the yard, with a drain running out under the building to a ditch outside. All of which is, I must admit, rather more clear in my mind than in the drawing.

## 73. A STAGE FOR *TITUS ANDRONICUS*

This is developed from the arrangement shown in Plate 70. The text demands, at stage level, two doors and the Tomb of the Andronici, which has to be opened to receive the coffin of Titus's sons. (There seems to be a disagreement among the texts as to whether there was one coffin or more.) Above is the Senate House. Here the play opens with the entrance of the Tribunes and Senators. These are joined later by Saturninus and Bassianus, who ascend to the Senate House from the stage, after a demand to 'open the gates and let me in'. So here is shown the Senate House aloft, with a canopy over the throne, the Tribunes and Senators seated, Saturninus and Bassianus, contenders for the throne, standing forward. Below, Titus Andronicus and Tamora, Queen of the Goths, and the other personages who appear in Peacham's sketch (Plate 45); and the coffin lying before the Tomb. This puts the matter in its plainest terms. Something like this it has to be.

I. LONDON FROM BANKSIDE, SHOWING THE GLOBE AND THE BEAR-GARDEN, *c.* 1616
From the engraving by J. C. Visscher

Old Swan
schrewesbury
howse.
The stilliarde

Three cranes
Quene hyth
Broken wharfe
Paules wharfe
Beynardes castle

Black friers
yde wel

friers

Temple
lo

Thamys
Fluuius

Banckes syde

south warke

S. Marye ouereys

Beare garden
The stare
The poude

The pounde

Swan          Bear-garden   Rose      Sts Mary Overies
                            Globe     (Southwark Cathedral)

2. BANKSIDE, SHOWING THE PLAYHOUSES, 1600
From John Norden's revised version of his earlier (1593) map of London

Convent garden     S. Clement

Arundel house

The Globe

Beere bayting

Barnards Castle

4. BANKSIDE SHOWING THE THEATRES (WIT

From the engravi

S. y.º Waterhouse

S. Andre in Holborne

S. Pauwls Church

Paules wharfe

Queene hythe

The 3 Cranes

the Eel Ships

Winchester house

(...IR NAMES REVERSED) SHORTLY BEFORE 1644

...nzel Hollar

5. ORIGINAL DRAWING OF THE SECOND GLOBE AND THE BEAR-GARDEN
BY WENZEL HOLLAR

*Bear-garden*        *Rose*        *Globe*

6. BANKSIDE, 1600

Detail from the *Civitas Londini* view

7. THE CURTAIN THEATRE, SHOREDITCH, *c.* 1600

Detail from *The View of the City of London from the North towards the South*

*The Globe on Bank Side Where Shakespere Acted*

8 and 9. DEBASED EIGHTEENTH-CENTURY VERSIONS OF THE GLOBE

THE FORTUNE PLAYHOUSE, GOLDEN LANE.

10. THE LAST DAYS OF THE FORTUNE THEATRE
Engraving by T. H. Shepherd, 1811

II. THE FORTUNE THEATRE: A RECONSTRUCTION, c. 1836

12. 'AN OLD ENGLISH INDOOR THEATRE', AS VISUALIZED IN 1836

13. THE GLOBE: A RECONSTRUCTION OF *c.* 1860

14. THE GLOBE: A RECONSTRUCTION OF 1910

15. AN OPENING FROM HENSLOWE'S DIARY FOR 1597-8

16. PORTION OF A LETTER FROM EDWARD ALLEYN TO HIS WIFE

The platt of The Secound parte of the Seuen Deadlie Sinns

A tent being plast one the stage for Henry the sixt he in it A sleepe to him The Leutenant A purceuant R Cowly Jo Duke and 1 wardere R Pallant to them Pride Gluttony wrath and Couetousnes at one dore at an other dore Enuie Sloth and Lechery The Three put back the foure and so Exeunt

Henry Awaking Enter A Keeper J Sincler to him a seruant T Belt to him Lidgate and the Keeper Exit then enter againe Then Enuy passeth ouer the stag Lidgate speakes

A senit Dumb show

Enter King Gorboduk wth 2 Counsailers R Burbadg mr Brian Th Goodale The Queene wth Ferrex and Porrex and som attendaunts follow Saunder wth Harry J Duke Kitt R Pallant J Holland After Gordbeduk hath Consulted wth his Lords he brings his 2 sonns to to seuerall seates They enving on on other Ferrex offers to take Porex his Corowne he drawes his weapon The King Queen and Lords step between them They Thrust them away and menasing ech other exit The Queene and Lords Depart Heauilie Lidgate speaks

Enter Ferrex Crownd wth Drum and Coulers and soldiers one way Harry Kitt R Cowly John duke to them At an other dore Porrex drum and Collers and sold wth W Sly R Pallant John Sincler J Holland

Enter Queene wth 2 Counsailors mr Brian Tho Goodale to them Ferrex and Porrex seuerall waies wth Drums and Powers Gorboduk entreing to the midst between Henry speaks

Alarum wth Excursions After Lidgate speakes

Enter Ferrex and Porrex seuerally Gorboduk still following them Lucius and Damasus wth Tho Good

Enter Ferrex at one dore Porrex at an other The fight Ferrex is slayn to them Videna the Queene to hir Damasus to him Lucius

Enter Porrex sad wth Dordan his man R P W Sly to them the Queene and A Ladie Nick Saunder and Lords R Cowly mr Brian to them Lucius Running

Henry and Lidgat speaks Sloth Passeth ouer

Enter Giraldus Phronesius Aspatia Pompeia Rodope R Cowly Th Goodale R Go Ned Nick

Enter Sardinapalus Arbactus Nicanor and Captaines marching mr Phillipps mr Pope R Pa Kit J Sincler J Holland

Enter A Captaine wth Aspatia and the Ladies Kitt

Lidgat speak

Enter Nicanor wth other Captaines R Pall J Sincler Kitt J Holland R Cowly to them Arbactus mr Pope to him will foole J Duke to him Rodopeie Ned to her Sardanapalus like A woman wth Aspatia Rodope Pompeia will foole to them Arbactus and 3 musitions mr Pope J Sincler Vincent R Cowly to them Nicanor and others R P Kitt

Enter Sardanapa wth the Ladies to them A Messenger Th Goodale to him will foole Running A Larum

Enter Arbactus pursuing Sardanapalus and the Ladies fly After Enter Sarda wth as many Jewels robes and Gold as he can cary

Alarum

Enter Arbactus Nicanor and the other Captains in triumph mr Pope R Pa Kitt J Holl R Cow J Sinc

Henry speaks and Lidgate Lechery passeth ouer the stag

Enter Tereus Philomele

R Burbadg

Enter Progne Itis and Lords Saunder will J Duke W Sly Harry

Enter Philomele and Tereus to them Julio

Enter Progne Panthea Itis and Lords Saunder T Belt will W Sly Harry Th Goodale to them Tereus wth Lords R Burbadg J Duk R Cowly

A Dumb show Lidgate speakes

Enter Progne wth the Sampler to her Tereus from Hunting wth his Lords to them Philomele wth Itis hed in a dish Mercury Comes and all Vanish to him 3 Lords Th Goodale Harry W Sly

Henry speaks to him Leiutenant Purceuant and warders R Cowly J Duke J Holland Joh Sincler to them Warwick mr Brian

Lidgate speaks to the Audiens and so Exitt

17. THE 'PLATT' OF THE SECOND PART OF *The Seuen Deadlie Sinns*

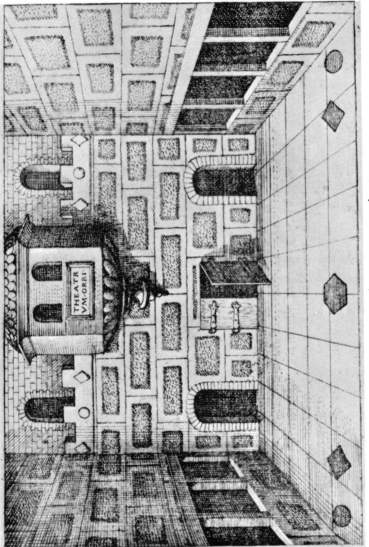

18. A MNEMONIC 'GLOBE THEATRE', 1619

19. THE STAGE FOR *Laurentius*, COLOGNE, 1581

20. PLAYERS IN AN AUDIENCE, NORTHERN ITALY, c. 1690

Painting attributed to Luca Carlevaris

21. THEATRE IN A MARKET PLACE, BRUSSELS, c. 1660
Painting by Adam van der Meulen

22. A MOUNTEBANK STAGE, *c.* 1600

23. A STREET THEATRE IN LOUVAIN, 1594

**24. CHRIST SHOWN TO THE PEOPLE**
Etching (1st state) by Rembrandt, 1655

**25. STAGE IN BRUSSELS, 1594**

ALDVS WAS HET TOONNEEL, STAENDE

26. THE TARQUIN STAGI

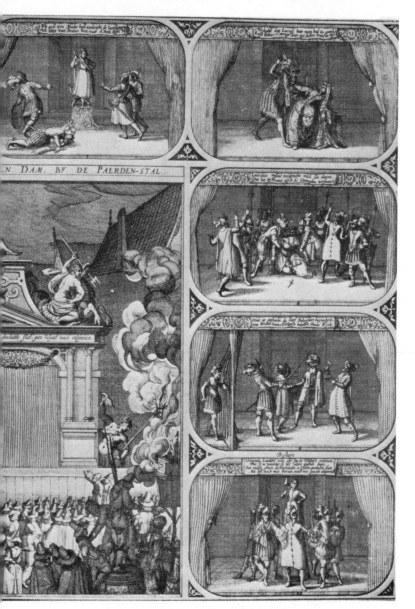

N DAM, BY DE PAERDEN-STAL

TERDAM, 1609

27. FLEMISH STREET THEATRE, 1607

28. BASQUE FOLK-DANCE STAGE, c. 1934

29. STREET THEATRE AND STROLLING PLAYERS, 1676

30. THE CAR OF THE NATIVITY: DETAIL FROM 'THE TRIUMPH OF ISABELLA', 1615

31. THE CAR OF ISABELLA AND HER COURT: DETAIL FROM 'THE TRIUMPH OF ISABELLA', 1615

ALST PAST,

BI APETITE.

GHĒDT.

33. STREET THEATRE, GHENT, 1539

32. *REDERYKER* STAGE AT ANTWERP, 1582

35. THE TRIUMPH OF JAMES I, LONDON,
1604: (2) THE TEMPLE OF JANUS

34. THE TRIUMPH OF JAMES I, LONDON,
1604: (1) THE FLEMISH ARCH

36. THE TRIUMPH OF JAMES I, LONDON, 1604: (3) THE ARCH OF LONDON

37. THE TRIUMPH OF JAMES I, LONDON, 1604: (4) THE GARDEN OF PLENTY

38. THE TRIUMPH OF JAMES I, LONDON, 1604: (5) THE NEW ARABIA FELIX

39. THE TRIUMPH OF JAMES I, LONDON, 1604: (6) THE ARCH OF THE NEW WORLD

40. THE CHARIOT OF ROYAL JUSTICE

41. THE ELVETHAM ENTERTAINMENT FOR QUEEN ELIZABETH I, 1591

42. FESTIVAL CAR AND COSTUMES, BRUNSWICK, 1616

43. BIOSCOPE ORGAN, ANTWERP, *c.* 1910

44. STAGING AT COURT, 1581

45. A SCENE FROM *TITUS ANDRONICUS*, *c.* 1595

46. COSTUMES IN THE ROMAN STYLE, *c.* 1611

47. JOHN SPEED'S TITLE-PAGE, 1614

48. BEN JONSON'S TITLE-PAGE, 1616

49. THE *MESSALLINA* TITLE-PAGE, 1640

50. THE *ROXANA* TITLE-PAGE, 1632

51. THE MERMAID THEATRE, LONDON, 1951

52. THE SCHOUWBURG, AMSTERDAM, 1658: THE AUDITORIUM

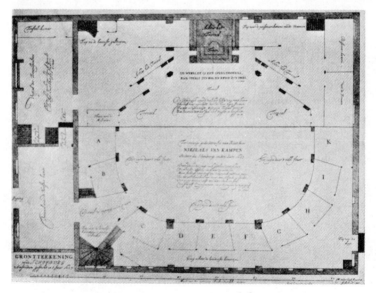

53. THE SCHOUWBURG, AMSTERDAM, 1658: GROUND-PLAN

54. THE SCHOUWBURG, AMSTERDAM, 1658: THE STAGE

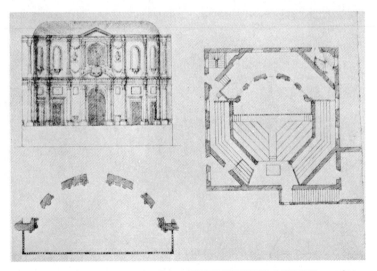

55. DESIGN FOR THE COCKPIT-IN-COURT THEATRE, LONDON, *c.* 1632

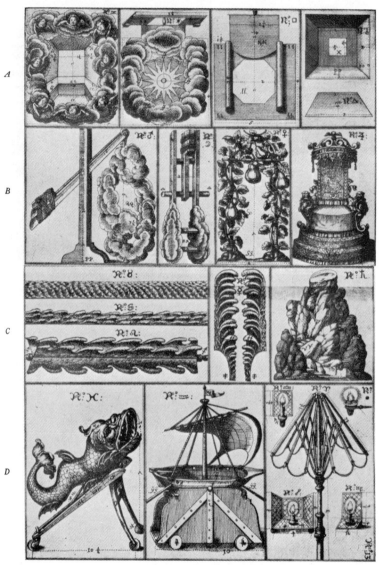

56. FURTENBACH'S THEATRICAL EFFECTS, 1663

57. INIGO JONES: A FANTASTIC ELEPHANT,

58. THE NORWICH DRAGON

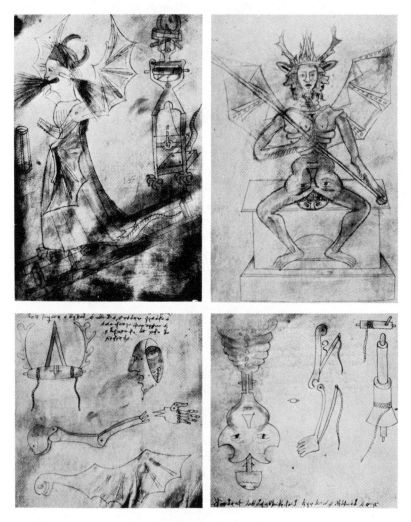

59. MECHANICAL DEVILS, FIFTEENTH CENTURY

60. THEATRICAL FLYING APPARATUS, SEVENTEENTH CENTURY

61. A JACOBEAN 'HEAVENS' AT CULLEN HOUSE, BANFFSHIRE

62. THE TROJAN WAR: CEILING AT CULLEN HOUSE, BANFFSHIRE, *c.* 1610

63. SIR HENRY UNTON'S WEDDING MASQUE, c. 1597

64. A LADY IN MASQUE COSTUME, *c.* 1610

65. INIGO JONES: AN OCEANID AS TORCHBEARER
Dress Design from the 'Masque of Blackness', 1605

66. INIGO JONES: IRIS

Dress Design from the masque 'Hymenaei', 1606

67. INIGO JONES: SCENERY FOR THE MASQUE OF 'OBERON', 1611

68. INIGO JONES: COSTUMES FOR THE MASQUE OF 'OBERON', 1611

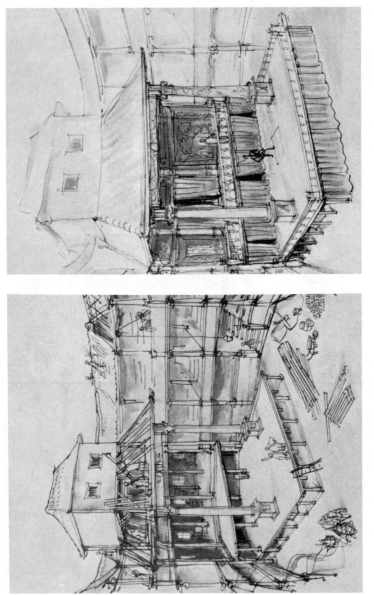

69. BUILDING A PLAYHOUSE

70. A CURTAINED TIRING-HOUSE

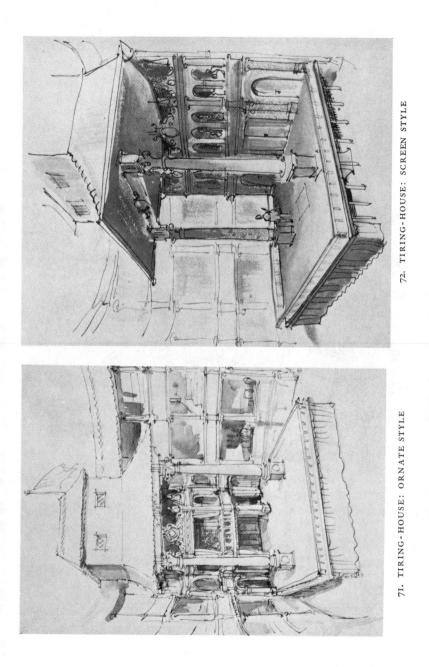

72. TIRING-HOUSE: SCREEN STYLE

71. TIRING-HOUSE: ORNATE STYLE

73. A STAGE FOR *TITUS ANDRONICUS*

# APPENDIXES

# APPENDIX A

## Reconstruction Sketches

I. STAGE IN AN INN-YARD, *c.* 1565

The stage shown here is based upon two pictures, one from the sixteenth century by Pieter Breughel the Younger, and the other from the seventeenth by Callot (see pp. ix and 33 of this book). The stages they show are almost identical. The sketch above is intended to represent a provincial fit-up. In the more firmly established conditions obtaining for a while at the great London inns this arrangement may have been modified somewhat, the stage perhaps being married up with the surrounding buildings, but the general effect was probably much the same.

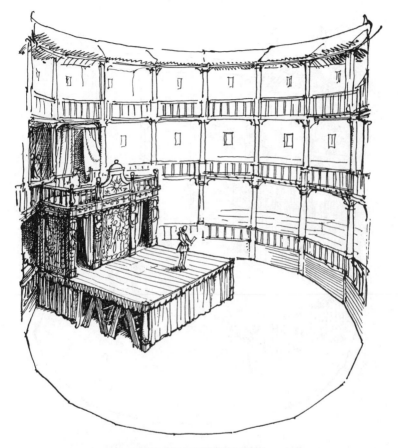

2. STAGE IN AN AMPHITHEATRE, *c.* 1576

The little stage and booth has now been moved into an arena, but it can be dismounted and removed if the yard is wanted for the 'game of bulls and bears'. When the stage is in position the galleries adjoining it are taken over as a back-stage area. The top of the booth has here been boarded over and railed in, so that it can be used as an acting place, and it is rather more elaborately decorated than formerly.

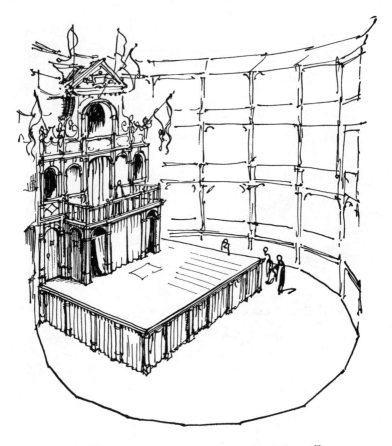

3. DEVELOPMENT OF A TIRING-HOUSE, 1580–90 (i)

This sketch and the following one represent possible intermediate steps in the early development of the theatres. The one above shows the direct line of development from the previous one (sketch 2). It is supposed that the stage has now become permanent. It has been enlarged, and stands no longer upon trestles but upon posts with curtains hung between. A stage trap can be seen. The booth, however, has here not enlarged itself, but remains as an individual enclosure within the structure that has grown up around it.

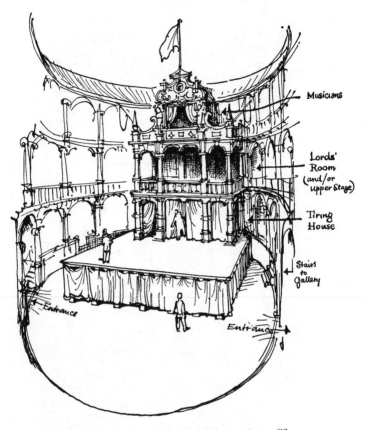

Musicians

Lords'
Room
(and/or
Upper Stage)

Tiring
House

Stairs
to
Gallery

Entrance

Entrance

**4. DEVELOPMENT OF A TIRING-HOUSE, 1580–90 (ii)**

This shows an alternative development. In this case it is assumed that the booth as well as the stage has been enlarged, built up, and ornamented in the Baroque style, as in the Flemish theatres. It may have been at this point that it became necessary to consider having a roof over the stage, partly to shelter the actors and stage furniture from the weather, partly perhaps to keep the afternoon sun out of the eyes of the audience, but chiefly to provide the spectacle of heavenly apparitions descending from above.

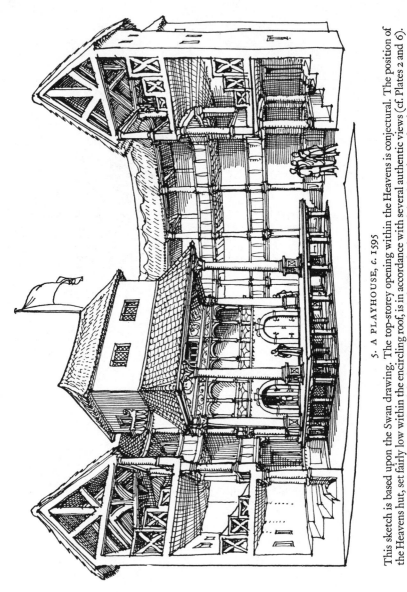

5. A PLAYHOUSE, c. 1595

This sketch is based upon the Swan drawing. The top-storey opening within the Heavens is conjectural. The position of the Heavens hut, set fairly low within the encircling roof, is in accordance with several authentic views (cf. Plates 2 and 6). The main weight of the hut is here carried upon the line of the tiring-house façade.

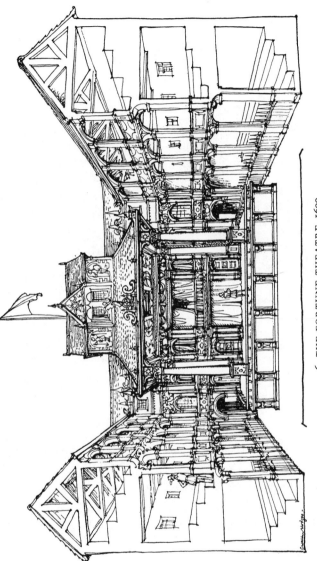

6. THE FORTUNE THEATRE, 1600

The over-all dimensions and layout are according to the contract, but details are necessarily conjectural. I here assume that the building was set with the tiring-house backing on to the street, and that the audience entered the yard along the gangways on either side of the stage. 'Iron pikes', as in the contract, are placed along the parapet of the bottom gallery to prevent persons from climbing over from the yard. Upper galleries are reached by stairs in the angles of the building near the street.

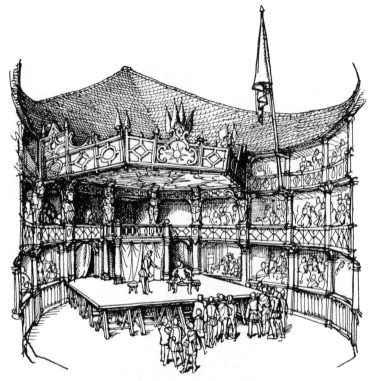

7. THE HOPE THEATRE, 1614

The discovery of the reversal of the names of the theatres in Hollar's view of Bankside (Plate 4) now enables us to reconstruct the conditions given in the Hope contract. The curious peak in the roof shown in the Hollar print indicates the way the builder solved his problem of constructing the Heavens 'without any posts or supporters' upon the stage. By raising the ridge-line on that side it was possible to give the inward-sloping members of the roof a long reach into and over the middle of the yard, thus supporting the Heavens from above as if by a sort of crane. Additional strength would be given to this by the fact of building on an interior curve. Since, however, the long lines of the roof overhanging the yard would have had a rather oppressive appearance, I suggest that this might have been minimized by erecting an ornamental fascia.

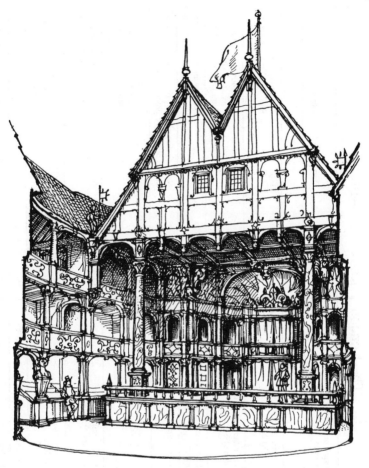

8. THE SECOND GLOBE, 1614

Following the Hollar print, I here show a greatly enlarged Heavens which, for stability, is now joined to the sides of the main building. This entails raising the ceiling to the height of the eaves, so as to avoid loss of light. I have also assumed that it may have been at this stage of theatre development that the traditional flat façade of the tiring-house began to give way to new influences, and I show a curved façade somewhat resembling the Cockpit drawing in Plate 55.

# APPENDIX B

## The London Theatres 1576–1660

| Theatre | Principal occupying companies | Managements | Built | Demolished | Remarks |
|---|---|---|---|---|---|
| *Public Theatres* | | | | | |
| THE THEATRE | The Chamberlain's (Lord Hunsdon's) Men | James Burbage and associates | 1576 | 1598 | The Queen's Men, with Richard Tarlton, sometimes acted here in the 1580s |
| THE CURTAIN | The Chamberlain's (Lord Hunsdon's) Men | Henry Lanman, sometimes in association with James Burbage | 1577–8 | Not heard of after 1627[1] | After 1603 this theatre became associated with Worcester's (later the Queen's) Men |
| NEWINGTON BUTTS | The Lord Admiral's Men and others | Philip Henslowe | ?1579 | ?1599 | Perhaps an unusually spacious upper stage (cf. page 53 above) |
| THE ROSE | The Lord Admiral's Men | Philip Henslowe | 1587 | Nothing directly known after 1605 | But tithes still due from the property in 1622 |
| THE SWAN | — | Francis Langley | c. 1594 | c. 1614 | Henslowe may have had an interest in it after Langley's death in 1601, but it seems not to have been much used |
| THE FORTUNE | The Lord Admiral's (later Prince Henry's) Men | Philip Henslowe and Edward Alleyn | 1600 | Dismantled 1649 | Destroyed by fire in 1621, but rebuilt 1623; finally demolished 1662 |
| THE GLOBE I | The Chamberlain's (later King's) Men | Cuthbert and Richard Burbage and associates (incl. Shakespeare) | 1599 | 1613 | Built with the timbers of the old Theatre Destroyed by fire |
| THE GLOBE II | The King's Men | ,, ,, | 1614 | 1644 | — |
| THE RED BULL | The Earl of Worcester's (the Queen's) Men | Aaron Holland and others | ?1606 | Last heard of in the 1660s | Altered or enlarged (roofed?) c. 1625 |

|  |  |  |  |  |  |
|---|---|---|---|---|---|
| THE HOPE | Lady Elizabeth's Men until 1615 | Philip Henslowe, Edward Alleyn, Jacob Meade | 1613-14 | 1656 | Built over the site of the original Bear-garden |
| *Private Theatres* |  |  |  |  |  |
| BLACKFRIARS I | Children of the Chapel (Queen's Revels) | Masters: William Hunnis Richard Farrant Henry Evans | 1576 | Converted 1584 | James Burbage leases and converts hall to theatre for own use in 1596, but does not then occupy. Leases to Evans and Giles in 1600, until 1608 |
| BLACKFRIARS II (*a*) | " " | Henry Evans, Nathaniel Giles | 1600 | 1608 |  |
| BLACKFRIARS II (*b*) | The King's Men | Cuthbert and Richard Burbage and associates | 1608 | 1655 | — |
| ST. PAUL'S | The Children of Paul's | Masters: Sebastian Westcott, d. 1582 1586 Thomas Giles 1599 Edward Peers | c. 1557 | c. 1608 | Acted at Court and sometimes at Blackfriars. Location of own house not known; it may have been the St. Paul's singing school, or else the Convocation House |
| WHITEFRIARS | Children of the King's Revels (composed from former children's companies?) | — | c. 1606 | 1629 | After 1609 Whitefriars occupied by different companies with indifferent success. After 1629 replaced by Salisbury Court. Replaced in Restoration times by Dorset Garden |
| SALISBURY COURT | Queen Henrietta's Men; Prince's Men | — | 1629 | 1649 |  |
| THE COCKPIT, DRURY LANE | The Earl of Worcester's (Queen Anne's) Men | Christopher Beeston | 1616 | c. 1666/7 | After its regular occupation as a playhouse began in 1616 this theatre was also known as the Phoenix |
| THE COCKPIT-IN-COURT | Visiting; three Shakespeare plays given here in 1639 | For courtly private occasions only | Converted for theatre c. 1604 | Not known | Rebuilt or remodelled in 1632 and again in 1666, but not heard of as a theatre after that date |

[1] Leslie Hotson (*Commonwealth and Restoration Stage*, p. 92) quotes a reference which seems to show that this theatre was still standing in 1660.

# APPENDIX C

A Juste a count of all suche money as J haue layd owt for my lord admeralles players
begyning the xj of octobr whose names ar as foloweth borne gabrell shaw Jonnes dowten
Jube towne synger & the ij geffes 1597

---

layd owt unto Robarte shawe to by a boocke for the companey the 21 of octobr 1597 the some of called the cobler   wittnes   E Alleyn } xxxx<sup>s</sup>

---

lent unto Robarte shaw to by a boocke of yonge harton the 5 of novembr 1597 the some of . . . wittnes   E Alleyn } x<sup>s</sup>

---

lent unto Robart shaw for the companey to bye viij yrdes of clothe of gow[e]lde for the womanes gowne in bran howlte the 26 of novembr 1597 the some of ..................... } iiij<sup>li</sup>

---

lent unto Robart shawe to geue the tayller to by tynsell for bornes gowne the j of desembr 1597   ix<sup>s</sup>

---

layd owt for the companye to by tafetie & tynssell for the bodeyes of a womanes gowne to play allce perce wch j dd unto the littel tayller the 8 desembre 1597 ......................... wittnes   E Alleyn } xx<sup>s</sup>

---

layd owt for mackynge allce perces bodeyes & a payer of yeare sleaues the some of ......... vj<sup>s</sup> vij<sup>d</sup>

---

lent unto Bengeman Johnson[1] the 3 of desembr 1597 upon a booke wch he showed the plotte vnto the company wch he promysed to dd vnto the company at cryssmas next the some of.... } xx<sup>s</sup>

---

lent unto Robart shawe to by copr lace of sylver for a payer of hosse in allce perce the 10 of desembr 1597........................................................................ witness wm borne Jube & gabrell spenser[2] } xvj<sup>a</sup>

---

layd owt for ij gyges for the companey to ij yonge men the 12 of desembr 1597 the some of   vj<sup>s</sup> 8<sup>d</sup>

---

layd owt the 22 of desembr 1597 for a boocke called mother Read cape to antony monday & drayton ................................................................................. } iiij<sup>li</sup>

---

layd owt the 28 of desembr 1597 for a boocke called mother Read cape to antoney mondaye   v<sup>s</sup>

---

lent the company to bye a flame coler satten dublett the 5 of Janeway 1597 the some of........ xxxx<sup>vs</sup>

---

[1] At this date Ben Jonson was known only as an actor and (with Nashe) part-author of *The Isle of Dogs*, a satirical play, now lost, which had caused great official displeasure. Indeed, it was only just two months before this entry of Henslowe's that Jonson was released from the Marshalsea prison, where he had been committed for his complicity in the play, both as actor and author. His first great success, *Every Man In His Humour*, did not come on to the stage till the September of the year following this entry, and then was put on by the Chamberlain's Men, Henslowe's competitors. The book referred to in this entry is not known, and it seems Jonson failed to deliver it.

[2] Gabriel Spenser's name appearing in this entry, following so close upon the reference to Ben Jonson, is interesting. At this time Spenser was one of Henslowe's best actors. Earlier he had shared imprisonment with Jonson over the *Isle of Dogs* affair (cf. footnote 1 above). But nine months after this diary entry (and incident-

# A typical opening from Henslowe's diary
(*See Plate 15*)

pd unto antony monday & drayton for the laste payment of the Boocke of mother Readcape the 5 of Janewary 1597 the some of............................................... } lv$^s$

for the littel boye
Layd owte for copr lace $\wedge$ & for a valle for the boye a geanste the playe of dido & eneus the 3 of Jenewary 1597. .................................................... } xxix$^s$

Lent vnto thomas dowton the 8 of Janewary 1597 twenty shillinges to by a boockes of mr dickers[1] lent ................................................................. } xx$^s$

Lent vnto the company when they fyrst played dido at nyght the some of thirtishillynges wch warse the 8 of Jeneway 1597 J saye ................................................ } xxx$^s$

lent vnto the company the 15 of Jeneway 1597[2] to bye a boocke of mr dicker called fayeton fower pownde J saye lent. ...................................................... } iiij$^{ll}$

lent vnto Thomas dowton for the company to bye a sewte for phayeton & ij Rebates & j fardengalle the 26 of Jeneway 1598 the some of three pownde J saye lent................. } iiij$^{ll}$

lent vnto Thomas dowton the 28 of Jeneway 1598 to bye a whitte satten dublett for phayeton fortyshyllenges J saye lent ...................................................... } xxxx$^s$

lent vnto the companey the 4 of febreary 1598 to dise charge my dicker owt of the cownter in the powltrey[3] the some of fortie shillinges J saye dd to thomas dowton.................... } xxxx$^s$

Layd owt vnto antony monday the 15 of febreary 1598 for a playe boocke called the firste parte of Robyne hoode............................................................... } v$^{ll}$

ally just two days after the first production of Jonson's *Every Man In His Humour*) he and Jonson quarrelled violently, and fought a duel in the fields at Shoreditch, near the Theatre. Spenser was slain outright, and Jonson was committed to prison once again. He was able to plead benefit of clergy, and so was eventually released with the forfeiture of his goods and with a branding on the thumb—the letter T, the felon's mark of Tyburn. On 26 September 1598 Henslowe wrote in a letter to his son-in-law, Edward Alleyn: 'Since you were with me I have lost one of my company, which hurteth me greatly, that is Gabriel, for he is slain in Hogsden Fields by the hands of Benjamin Jonson. . . .'

[1] *Mr. Dicker* = Thomas Dekker, the playwright.
[2] Note that although the new year is already a fortnight old, Henslowe is still writing 1597 instead of 1598!
[3] *The Counter in the Poultry.* A prison where Dekker appears to have been detained for debt.

# APPENDIX D

## The Platt of the Secound Parte of the Seuen Deadlie Sinns

*(See Plate 17)*

---

A TENT being plast on the stage for Henry the Sixt. He in it asleepe. To him the Lieu-tenenant, a Purcevant, R. Cowley Jo Duke, & 1 Warder, R. Pallant. to them Pride, Gluttony, Wrath and Covetousnes at one dore. at another dore Envie, Sloth and Lechery. The three put back the foure and so exeunt.

---

Henry awaking Enter a Keeper J. Sincler. to him a Servaunt T. Belt to him Lidgate, & the Keeper Exit. then enter againe. Then Envy passeth over the stag. Lidgate speakes.

---

A Senitt. Dumb show.

Enter King Gorboduk w^th Counsailers. R. Burbadg Mr Brian Th. Goodale. The Queene with Ferrex and Porrex and som attendaunts follow. Saunder. W. Sly. Harry. J. Duke, Kitt. R° Pallant. J. Holland. After Gorboduk hath consulted with his lords he brings his 2 sonns to several seates. They *enving* on on other Ferrex offers to take Porex his Corowne. he draws his weapon. The King Queene and Lords step betweene them. They thrust them away and menasing ech other exit. The Queene and Lords depart hevilie. Lidgate speakes.

---

Enter Ferrex crownd with drum & coulers and soldiers one way. Harry. Kitt. R. Cowley John Duke. to them at another dore Porrex drum & collors & soldiers. W. Sly, R. Pallant. John Sincler, J. Holland.

---

Enter queene with 2 counsailors Mr. Brian Tho Goodale. to them Ferrex and Porrex several waies with drums and powers. Gorboduk entering in the midst between. Henry speaks.

---

Alarums with excurtions. After Lidgate speakes.

---

Enter Ferrex and Porrex severally Gorboduk still following them. Lucius Damasus Mr. Bry T. Good.

---

Enter Ferrex at one dore. Porrex at another. The fight. Ferrex is slayne. To them Videna the Queene. to her Damasus. to him Lucius.

---

Enter Porrex sad with Dordan his man. R.P.W. Sly. To them the Queene and a Ladie. Nich. Saunder. and Lords R. Cowly Mr. Brian. To them Lucius running.

---

Henry and Lidgat speaks. Sloth passeth over.

---

Enter Giraldus Phronesius Aspatia Pompeia Rodope. R. Cowly. Th. Goodale. R. Go. Ned. Nick.

---

Enter Sardinapalus Arbactus Nicanor and Captaines marching. Mr. Phillipps, Mr. Pope, R. Pa. Kit. J. Sincler. J. Holland.

---

Enter a Captaine with Aspatia and the Ladies. Kitt.

---

Lidgat speake.
Enter Nicanor w[th] other Captaines R. Pall. J. Sincler. Kitt. J. Holland. R. Cowly. to them Arbactus Mr. Pope. to him Will Foole J. Duke. to him Rodopeie Ned. to her Sardanapalus like a woman with Aspatia Rodope Pompeia Will. Foole. to them Arbactus & 3 musitions Mr. Pope J. Sincler. Vincent. R. Cowly. to them Nicanor and others R. P. Kitt.

---

Enter Sardanapa. w[th] the Ladies. to them a Messenger Tho Goodale. to him Will Foole running. Alarum.

---

Enter Arbactus pursuing Sardanapalus. and the Ladies fly. After enter Sarda. with as many jewels robes and gold as he can cary.
                    Alarum.

---

Enter Arbactus Nicanor and the other Captains in triumph. Mr. Pope R. Pa. Kitt J. Holl. R. Cow. J. Sinc.

---

Henry speakes and Lidgate. Lechery passeth over the stag.

---

Enter Tereus Philomela Julio. R. Burbadge Ro. R. Pall. J. Sink.

---

Enter Progne Itis and Lords. Saunder. Will. J. Duke. W. Sly. Harry.

---

Enter Philomele and Tereus, to them Julio.

---

Enter Progne Panthea Itis amd Lords. Sander. T. Belt. Will. W. Sly. Hary. Th. Goodale. to them Tereus with Lords R. Burbadge. J. Duk. R. Cowley.

---

A dumb show. Lidgate speaks.

Enter Progne with the sampler. to her Tereus from hunting w^th his Lords to them Philomele with Itis hed in a dish. Mercury comes and all vanish. to him 3 Lords. Th. Goodale. Harey. W. Sly.

---

Henry speaks to him Lieutenant Pursevaunt and Warders. R. Cowley J. Duke J. Holland. Joh. Sincler. to them Warwick Mr. Brian.

---

Lidgate speaks to the audiens and so Exitts.

# APPENDIX E

## The Plot of the Play called England's Joy

To be played at the Swan this 6 of November, 1602.

FIRST, there is induct by show and in action, the civil wars of England from Edward the Third to the end of Queen Mary's reign, with the overthrow of usurpation.

2. Secondly then the entrance of England's Joy by the Coronation of our Sovereign Lady Elizabeth; her Throne attended with Peace, Plenty and Civil Policy: a sacred prelate standing at her right hand, betokening the serenity of the Gospel; at her left hand Justice; and at her feet War, with a scarlet robe of peace upon his armour; a wreath of bays about his temples, and a branch of palm in his hand.

3. Thirdly is dragged in three Furies, presenting Dissension, Famine, and Bloodshed, which are thrown into hell.

4. Fourthly is expressed under the person of a Tyrant, the envy of Spain, who to show his cruelty, causeth his soldiers drag in a beautiful Lady, whom they mangle and wound, tearing her garments and jewels from off her; and so leave her bloody, with her hair about her shoulders, lying upon the ground. To her come certain gentlemen, who seeing her piteous despoilment, turn to the Throne of England, from whence one descendeth, taketh up the Lady, wipeth her eyes, bindeth up her wounds, giveth her treasure, and bringeth forth a band of soldiers, who attend her forth. This Lady presenteth Belgia.

5. Fifthly, the Tyrant more enraged, taketh counsel, sends forth letters, privy spies and secret underminers, taking their oaths and giving them bags of treasure. These signify Lopus,[1] and certain Jesuits, who afterward, when the Tyrant looks for an answer from them, are showed to him in a glass with halters about their necks, which makes him mad with fury.

6. Sixthly, the Tyrant, seeing all secret means to fail him, intendeth upon violence and invasion by the hand of War, whereupon is set forth the battle at Sea in '88, with Englands victory.

---

[1] *Lopus.* Doctor Ruy Lopez, an elderly physician popularly supposed to have been involved in a plot to poison the Queen. He was executed at Tyburn in 1594.

7. Seventhly, he complotteth with the Irish rebels, wherein is laid open the base ingratitude of Tyrone, the landing there of Don John de Aguila, and their dissipation by the wisdom and valour of the Lord Mountjoy.

8. Eighthly, a great triumph is made with fighting of twelve gentlemen at Barriers, and sundry rewards sent from the Throne of England, to all sorts of well deservers.

9. Lastly, the Nine Worthies, with several coronets, present themselves before the Throne, which are put back by certain in the habit of Angels, who set upon the Lady's head which represents her Majesty, an Imperial Crown, garnished with the sun, moon and stars. And so with music both with voice and instruments she is taken up into Heaven, when presently appears a Throne of blessed souls, and beneath under the stage set forth with strange fireworks, divers black and damned souls, wonderfully described in their several torments.

[*Note*: The foregoing is the full text of a playbill, though whether or not there was ever a play to support it is open to question. The author of the bill, Richard Venner, claimed in after years that there had been one, but that just before it was due to begin he was intercepted by bailiffs who 'seizing me before the first entrance, spoke an Epilogue instead of a Prologue'. At all events, nothing went on to the stage and the occasion itself became a byword. Even ten years later, in *Love Restored*, Jonson speaks of a 'fine trick, a piece of England's Joy'. What happened that day at the Swan is told in a letter written by John Chamberlain:

And, now we are in mirth, I must not forget to tell you of a cozening prank of one Venner, of Lincoln's Inn, that gave out bills of a famous play on Saturday was sevennight on the Bankside, to be acted only by certain gentlemen and gentlewomen of account. The price at coming in was two shillings or eighteen pence at least; and, when he had gotten most part of the money into his hands, he would have showed them a fair pair of heels, but he was not so nimble to get up on horseback, but that he was fain to forsake that course, and betake himself to the water, where he was pursued and taken, and brought before the Lord Chief Justice, who would make nothing of it but a jest and a merriment, and bound him over in five pound to appear at the sessions. In the mean time the common people, when they saw themselves deluded, revenged themselves upon the hangings, curtains, chairs, stools, walls and whatsoever came in their way, very outrageously, and made great spoil; there was great store of good company and many noblemen.]

# APPENDIX F

## The Contract for Building the Fortune Theatre, 1599

(From the text given by Dr. W. W. Greg in 'The Henslowe Papers' in
*Dramatic Documents from the Elizabethan Playhouses*)

THIS Indenture made the Eighte daie of Januarye 1599, and in the Twoe and Fortyth yeare of the Reigne of our sovereigne Ladie Elizabeth, by the grace of god Queene of Englande, Fraunce and Irelande, defender of the Faythe, &c. betwene Phillipp Henslowe and Edwarde Allen of the parishe of Sᵗᵉ Saviours in Southwark in the Countie of Surrey, gentlemen, on thone parte, and Peeter Streete, Cittizen and Carpenter of London, on thother parte witnesseth That whereas the saide Phillipp Henslowe & Edward Allen, the daie of the date hereof, haue bargayned, compounded & agreed with the saide Peter Streete ffor the erectinge, buildinge & settinge upp of a new howse and Stadge for a Plaiehouse in and vppon a certeine plott or parcell of grounde appoynted oute for that purpose, scytuate and beinge nere Goldinge lane in the parishe of Sᵗᵉ Giles withoute Cripplegate of London, to be by him the saide Peeter Streete or somme other sufficyent woorkmen of his provideinge and appoyntemente and att his propper costes & chardges, for the consideracion hereafter in theis presentes expressed, made, erected, builded and sett upp in manner & forme followinge (that is to saie); The frame of the saide howse to be sett square and to conteine ffowerscore foote of lawfull assize everye waie square with-one foote of assize att the leiste aboue the grounde; And the saide fframe to conteine three stronge foundacion of pyles, brick, lyme and sand bothe without & within, to be wroughte one foote of assize att the leiste aboue the grounde; And the saide flrame to conteine three Stories in heighth, the first or lower Storie to conteine Twelue foote of lawfull assize in heighth, the second Storie Eleauen foote of lawfull assize in heigth, and the third or vpper Storie to conteine Nyne foote of lawfull assize in height; All which Stories shall conteine Twelue foote and a halfe of lawfull assize in breadth througheoute, besides a juttey forwardes in either of the saide twoe vpper Stories of Tenne ynches of lawfull assize, with ffower convenient divisions for gentlemens roomes, and other sufficient and convenient divisions for Twoe pennie roomes, with necessarie seates to be placed and sett, aswell in those roomes as througheoute all the rest of the galleries of the saide howse, and with suchelike steares, conveyances & divisions withoute & within, as are made & contryved in and to the late erected Plaiehowse on the Banck in the saide parishe of Sᵗᵉ Saviours called the Globe; With a Stadge and Tyreinge howse to be made, erected & settupp within the saide flrame, with a shadowe or cover over the saide Stadge, which

Stadge shalbe placed & sett, as alsoe the stearecases of the saide fframe, in suche sorte as is prefigured in a plott thereof drawen,[1] and which Stadge shall conteine in length Fortie and Three foote of lawfull assize and in breadth to extende to the middle of the yarde of the saide howse; The same Stadge to be paled in belowe with good, stronge and sufficyent

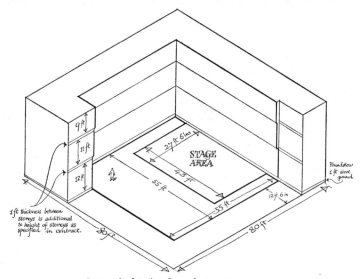

Isometric drawing from the Fortune contract

newe oken bourdes, and likewise the lower Storie of the saide fframe withinside, and the same lower storie to be alsoe laide over and fenced with stronge yron pykes; And the saide Stadge to be in all other proporcions contryved and fashioned like vnto the Stadge of the saide Plaie howse called the Globe; With convenient windowes and lightes glazed to the saide Tyreinge howse; And the saide fframe, Stadge and Stearecases to be covered with Tyle, and to haue a sufficient gutter of lead to carrie & convey the water frome the coveringe of the saide Stadge to fall backwardes; And also all the saide fframe and the Staircases thereof to be sufficyently enclosed withoute with lathe, lyme & haire, and the gentlemens roomes and Twoe pennie roomes to be seeled with lathe, lyme & haire, and all the fflowers of the saide Galleries, Stories and Stadge to be bourded with good & sufficyent newe deale bourdes of the whole thicknes, wheare need shalbe; And the saide howse and other thinges beforemencioned to be made & doen to be in all other contrivitions, conveyances, fashions, thinge and thinges effected, finished and doen accordinge to

[1] This 'plott' does not now exist.

the manner and fashion of the saide howse called the Globe, saveinge only that all the princypall and maine postes of the saide fframe and Stadge forwarde shalbe square and wroughte palasterwise, with carved proporcions called Satiers to be placed & sett on the topp of every of the same postes, and saveinge alsoe that the said Peeter Streete shall not be chardged with anie manner of pay[ntin]ge in or aboute the saide fframe howse or Stadge or anie parte thereof, nor rendringe the walls within, nor seeling anie more or other roomes then the gentlemens roomes, Twoe pennie roomes and Stadge before remembred. Nowe theiruppon the saide Peeter Streete dothe covenant, promise and graunte ffor himself, his executours and administratours, to and with the saide Phillipp Henslowe and Edward Allen and either of them, and thexecutours and administratours of them and either of them, by theis presentes in manner & forme followeinge (that is to saie); That he the saide Peeter Streete, his executours or assignes, shall & will att his or their owne propper costes & chardges well, woorkmanlike & substancyallie make, erect, sett upp and fully finishe in and by all thinges, accordinge to the true meaninge of theis presentes, with good, stronge and substancyall newe tymber and other necessarie stuff, all the saide fframe and other woorkes whatsoever in and vppon the saide plott or parcell of grounde (beinge not by anie aucthoretie restrayned, and haveinge ingres, egres & regres to doe the same) before the ffyue & twentith daie of Julie next commeinge after the date hereof; And shall alsoe at his or theire like costes and chardges provide and finde all manner of woorkmen, tymber, joystes, rafters, boordes, dores, boltes, hinges, brick, tyle, lathe, lyme, haire, sande, nailes, lade, iron, glasse, woorkmanshipp and other thinges whatsoever, which shalbe needefull, convenyent & necessarie for the saide fframe & woorkes & euerie parte thereof; And shall alsoe make all the saide fframe in every poynte for Scantlinges lardger and bigger in assize then the Scantlinges of the timber of the saide newe erected howse called the Globe; And alsoe that he the saide Peeter Streete shall furthwith, aswell by himself as by suche other and soemanie woorkmen as shalbe convenient & necessarie, enter into and vppon the saide buildinges and woorkes, and shall in reasonable manner proceede therein withoute anie wilfull detraccion vntill the same shalbe fully effected and finished. In consideracion of all which buildinges and of all stuff & woorkemanshipp thereto belonginge, the saide Phillipp Henslowe & Edward Allen and either of them, ffor themselues, theire, and either of theire executours & administratours, doe joynctlie & seuerallie covenante & graunte to & with the saide Peeter Streete, his executours & administratours by theis presentes, that they the saide Phillipp Henslowe & Edward Allen or one of them, or the executours administratours or assignes of them or one of them, shall & will well & truelie paie or cawse to be paide vnto the saide Peeter Streete, his executours or assignes, att the place aforesaid appoynted for the erectinge of the saide fframe, the full somme of Fower hundred & Fortie Poundes of lawfull money of Englande in manner & forme followeinge (that is to saie), att suche tyme and when as the Tymberwoork of the saide fframe shalbe rayzed & sett upp by the saide Peeter Streete his executours or assignes, or within seaven daies then next followeinge, Twoe hundred & Twentie poundes, and att suche time and when as the saide fframe & woorkes shalbe fullie effected & ffynished as is aforesaide, or within seaven daies then next followeinge, thother Twoe hundred and Twentie poundes, withoute fraude or coven. Prouided allwaies, and it is agreed betweene the saide parties, that whatsoever somme or sommes of money the saide Phillipp Henslowe & Edward Allen or either of them, or thexecutours or assignes of them or either of them, shall lend or deliver vnto the saide Peter Streete his executours or assignes, or anie other by his appoyntemente or consent, ffor or concerninge the saide woorkes or anie parte thereof or anie stuff thereto belonginge, before the razeinge & settinge upp of the saide fframe, shalbe reputed, accepted, taken & accoumpted in parte of the firste pay-mente aforesaid of the saide some of Fower hundred & Fortie poundes, and all suche somme & sommes of money, as they or anie of them shall as aforesaid lend or deliver betwene the razeinge of the saide fframe & finishinge thereof and of all the rest of the saide woorkes, shalbe reputed, accepted, taken & accoumpted in parte of the laste pamente aforesaid of the same somme of Fower hundred & Fortie poundes, anie thinge abouesaid to the contrary notwithstandinge. In witnes whereof the parties abouesaid to theis pre-sente Indentures Interchaungeably haue sett theire handes and seales. Yeoven the daie and yeare ffirste abouewritten.

P S

Sealed and deliuered by the saide Peter Streete in the presence of me William Harris Pub[lic] Scr[ivener] And me Frauncis Smyth appr[entice] to the said Scr[ivener]

[Endorsed:] Peater Streat ffor The Building of the Fortune.

# APPENDIX G

# The Contract for Building the Hope Theatre, 1613

(From the text given by Dr. W. W. Greg in 'The Henslowe Papers')

ARTICLES, Covenauntes, grauntes, and agreementes, Concluded and agreed vppon this Nyne and Twenteithe daie of Auguste, Anno Domini 1613, Betwene Phillipe Henslowe of the parishe of S$^t$ Saviour in Sowthworke within the countye of Surrey, Esquire, and Jacobe Maide of the parishe of S$^t$ Olaves in Sowthworke aforesaide, waterman, of thone partie, And Gilbert Katherens of the saide parishe of S$^t$ Saviour in Sowthworke, Carpenter, on thother partie, As followeth, That is to saie—

Inprimis the saide Gilbert Katherens for him, his executours, administratours, and assignes, dothe convenaunt, promise, and graunt to and with the saide Phillipe Henslowe and Jacobe Maide and either of them, thexecutors, administratours, & assigns of them and either of them, by theise presentes in manner and forme following: That he the saied Gilbert Katherens, his executours, administratours, or assignes shall and will, at his or theire owne proper costes and charges, vppon or before the last daie of November next ensuinge the daie of the date of theise presentes above written, not onlie take downe or pull downe all that same place or house wherin Beares and Bulls haue been heretofore vsuallie bayted, and also one other house or staple wherin Bulls and horsses did vsuallie stande, sett, lyinge, and beinge vppon or neere the Banksyde in the saide parishe of S$^t$ Saviour in Sowthworke, comonlie called or knowne by the name of the Beare garden, but shall also at his or theire owne proper costes and charges vppon or before the saide laste daie of November newly erect, builde, and sett vpp one other same place or Plaie-house fitt & convenient in all thinges, bothe for players to playe in, and for the game of Beares and Bulls to be bayted in the same, and also a fitt and convenient Tyre house and a stage to be carryed or taken awaie, and to stande vppon tressells good, substanciall, and sufficient for the carryinge and bearinge of suche a stage; And shall new builde, erect, and sett vp againe the saide plaie house or game place neere or vppon the saide place, where the saide game place did heretofore stande; And to builde the same of suche large compasse, fforme, widenes, and height as the Plaie house called the Swan in the libertie of Parris garden in the saide parishe of S$^t$ Saviour now is; And shall also builde two steare-casses without and adioyninge to the saide Playe house in suche convenient places, as shalbe moste fitt and convenient for the same to stande vppon, and of such largnes and height as the stearecasses of the saide playehouse called the Swan nowe are or bee; And shall also builde the Heavens all over the saide stage, to be borne or carryed without any postes or supporters to be fixed or sett vppon the saide stage, and all gutters of leade needfull for the carryage of all suche raine water as shall fall vppon the same; And shall also make two Boxes in the lowermost storie fitt and decent for gentlemen to sitt in; And shall make the particions betwne the Rommes as they are at the saide Plaie house called the Swan; And to make turned cullumes vppon and over the stage; And shall make the principalls and fore fronte of the saide Plaie house of good and sufficient oken tymber, and no furr tymber to be putt or vsed in the lower most, or midell stories, except the vpright postes on the backparte of the saide stories (all the byndinge joystes to be of oken tymber); The inner principall postes of the first storie to be twelve footes in height and tenn ynches square, the inner principall postes in the midell storie to be eight ynches square, the inner most postes in the vpper storie to be seaven ynches square; The prick postes in the first storie to be eight ynches square, in the seconde storie seaven ynches square, and in the vpper most storie six ynches square; Also the brest sommers in the lower moste storie to be nyne ynches depe, and seaven ynches in thicknes, and in the midell storie to be eight ynches depe and six ynches in thicknes; The byndinge jostes of the firste storie to be nyne and eight ynches in depthe and thicknes, and in the midell storie to be viij and vij ynches in depthe and thicknes. Item to make a good, sure, and sufficient found-acion of brickes for the saide Play house or game place, and to make it xiij<sup>teene</sup> ynches at the leaste above the grounde. Item to new builde, erect, and sett vpp the saide Bull house and stable with good and sufficient scantlinge tymber, plankes, and bordes, and particions of that largnes and fittnes as shalbe sufficient to kepe and holde six bulls and three horsses or geldinges, with rackes and mangers to the same, and also a lofte or storie over the saide house as nowe it is. And shall also at his & theire owne proper costes and charges new tyle with Englishe tyles all the vpper rooffe of the saide Plaie house, games place, and Bull house or stable, and shall fynde and paie for at his like proper costes and charges for all the lyme, heare, sande, brickes, tyles, lathes, nayles, workemanshipe and all other thinges need-full and necessarie for the full finishinge of the saide Plaie house, Bull house, and stable; And the saide Plaiehouse or game place to be made in althinges and in suche forme and fashion, as the saide plaie house called the Swan (the scantling of the tymbers, tyles, and foundacion as ys aforesaide without fraude or coven). And the saide Phillipe Henslow and Jacobe Maide and either of them for them, thexecutors, administratours, and assignes of them and either of them, doe covenant and graunt to and with the saide Gilbert Katherens, his executours, administratours, and assignes in manner and forme followinge (That is to saie) That he the saide Gilbert or his assignes shall or maie haue, and take to his or theire vse and behoofe, not onlie all the tymber, benches, seates, slates, tyles, brickes, and all other thinges belonginge to the saide Game place & Bull house or stable, and also all suche olde tymber whiche the saide Phillipe Henslow hathe latelie bought, beinge of an old house in Thames street, London, whereof moste parte is now lyinge in the yarde or backsyde of the saide Bearegarden; And also to satisfie and paie vnto the saide Gilbert

Katherens, his executors, administratours, or assignes for the doinge and finishinges of
the workes and buildinges aforesaid the somme of Three Hundered and three score
poundes of good and lawffull monie of England, in manner and forme followinge (That is
to saie) In hande at thensealinge and deliuery hereof, Three score pounds which the saide
Gilbert acknowledgeth him selfe by theise presentes to haue receaued; And more over to
paie every weeke weeklie, duringe the firste six weekes, vnto the saide Gilbert or his
assignes, when he shall sett workemen to worke vppon or about the buildinge of the
premisses the somme of Tenne poundes of lawffull monie of Englande to paie them there
wages (yf theire wages dothe amount vnto somuche monie); And when the saide plaie
house, Bull house, and stable are reared, then to make vpp the saide wages one hundred
poundes of lawffull monie of England, and to be paide to the saide Gilbert or his assignes;
And when the saide Plaie house, Bull house, and stable are Reared, tyled, walled, then to
paie vnto the saide Gilbert Katherens or his assignes one other hundered poundes of
lawffull monie of England; And when the saide Plaie house, Bull house, and stable are
fullie finished, builded, and done in manner and forme aforesaide, then to paie vnto the
saide Gilbert Katherens or his assignes one other hundred Poundes of lawffull monie of
England in full satisfacion and payment of the saide somme of CClx[11]. And to all and
singuler the covenantes, grauntes, articles, and agreementes above in theise presentes
contayned, whiche on the parte and behalfe of the saide Gilbert Katherens, his executours,
administratours, or assignes are ought to be observed, performed, fulfilled, and done, the
saide Gilbert Katherens byndeth himselfe, his executours, administratours, and assignes
vnto the saide Phillipe Henslowe and Jacob Maide and to either of them, thexecutours,
administratours, and assignes of them or either of them, by theise presentes. In witnes
whereof the saide Gilbert Katherens hath herevnto sett his hande and seale, the daie and
yere firste above written

The mark G K of Gilbert Katherens

Sealed and Deliuered in the presence of
witnes Moyses Bowler
        Edwarde Griffin

# SELECT BIBLIOGRAPHY

ADAMS, JOHN CRANFORD. *The Globe Playhouse: Its Design and Equipment*. Cambridge, Mass., 1942.

BECKERMAN, BERNARD. *Shakespeare at the Globe*. New York, 1962.

BENTLEY, GERALD EADES. *The Jacobean and Caroline Stage*, 5 vols. Oxford, 1941–56.

BERNHEIMER, RICHARD. 'Another Globe Theatre', *Shakespeare Quarterly*, Winter 1958.

CAMPBELL, LILY B. *Scenes and Machines on the English Stage during the Renaissance*. Cambridge, 1923; 2nd ed., London, 1961.

CHAMBERS, E. K. *The Elizabethan Stage*, 4 vols. Oxford, 1923.

CREIZENACH, W. *The English Drama in the Age of Shakespeare*. Berlin and Stuttgart, 1916.

GRANVILLE-BARKER, HARLEY, and HARRISON, G. B. (eds.). *A Companion to Shakespeare Studies*. Cambridge, 1934.

GRAVES, T. S. *The Court and the London Theatres during the Reign of Queen Elizabeth*. 1913.

GREG, W. W. *Dramatic Documents from the Elizabethan Playhouses*, 2 vols. Oxford, 1931.

HARRISON, G. B. *Introducing Shakespeare*. London, 1939; 2nd ed., London, 1967.

HOSLEY, RICHARD. 'The Discovery Space in Shakespeare's Globe', *Shakespeare Survey 12*, 1959.

—— 'The Gallery over the Stage in the Public Playhouse of Shakespeare's Time', *Shakespeare Quarterly*, Winter 1957.

HOTSON, LESLIE. *Shakespeare's Wooden O*. London, 1959.

JOSEPH, B. L. *Elizabethan Acting*. Oxford, 1951; 2nd ed., Oxford, 1964.

KERNODLE, GEORGE R. *From Art to Theatre*. Chicago, 1944.

LAWRENCE, W. J. *The Physical Conditions of the Elizabethan Public Playhouse*. Cambridge, Mass., 1927.

—— *The Elizabethan Playhouse*, 2 vols. Stratford-on-Avon, 1912, 1913.

—— *Pre-Restoration Stage Studies*. Cambridge, Mass., 1927.

NAGLER, A. M. *Shakespeare's Stage*. New Haven, Conn., 1958.

NICOLL, ALLARDYCE. *The Development of the Theatre*. London, 1928; 5th ed., London, 1966.

—— *Stuart Masques and the Renaissance Stage*. London, 1937.

REYNOLDS, G. F. *The Staging of Elizabethan Plays at the Red Bull Theatre, 1605–1625*. New York, 1940.

ROEDER-BAUMBACH, IRMENGARD VON. *Versieringen bij Blijde Inkomsten*. Antwerp, 1943.

SOUTHERN, RICHARD. *The Open Stage*. London, 1953.

—— *The Mediaeval Theatre in the Round*. London, 1957.

—— 'On Reconstructing a Practicable Elizabethan Playhouse', *Shakespeare Survey 12*, 1959.

—— *The Seven Ages of the Theatre*. London, 1962.

SMITH, IRWIN. *Shakespeare's Globe Playhouse*. New York, 1956.

—— *Shakespeare's Blackfriars Playhouse*. New York, 1964; London, 1966.

SPEAIGHT, ROBERT. *William Poel and the Elizabethan Revival*. London, 1954.

THORNDIKE, ASHLEY H. *Shakespeare's Theatre*. New York, 1916.

WATKINS, RONALD. *On Producing Shakespeare*. London, 1950.

WICKHAM, GLYNNE. *Early English Stages*, 2 vols. London, 1963.

# INDEX

# NORTON CRITICAL EDITIONS